TABLIGHI JAMAAT

IDEOLOGY AND ORGANISATIONAL STRUCTURE

RAMEEZ AHMAD LONE

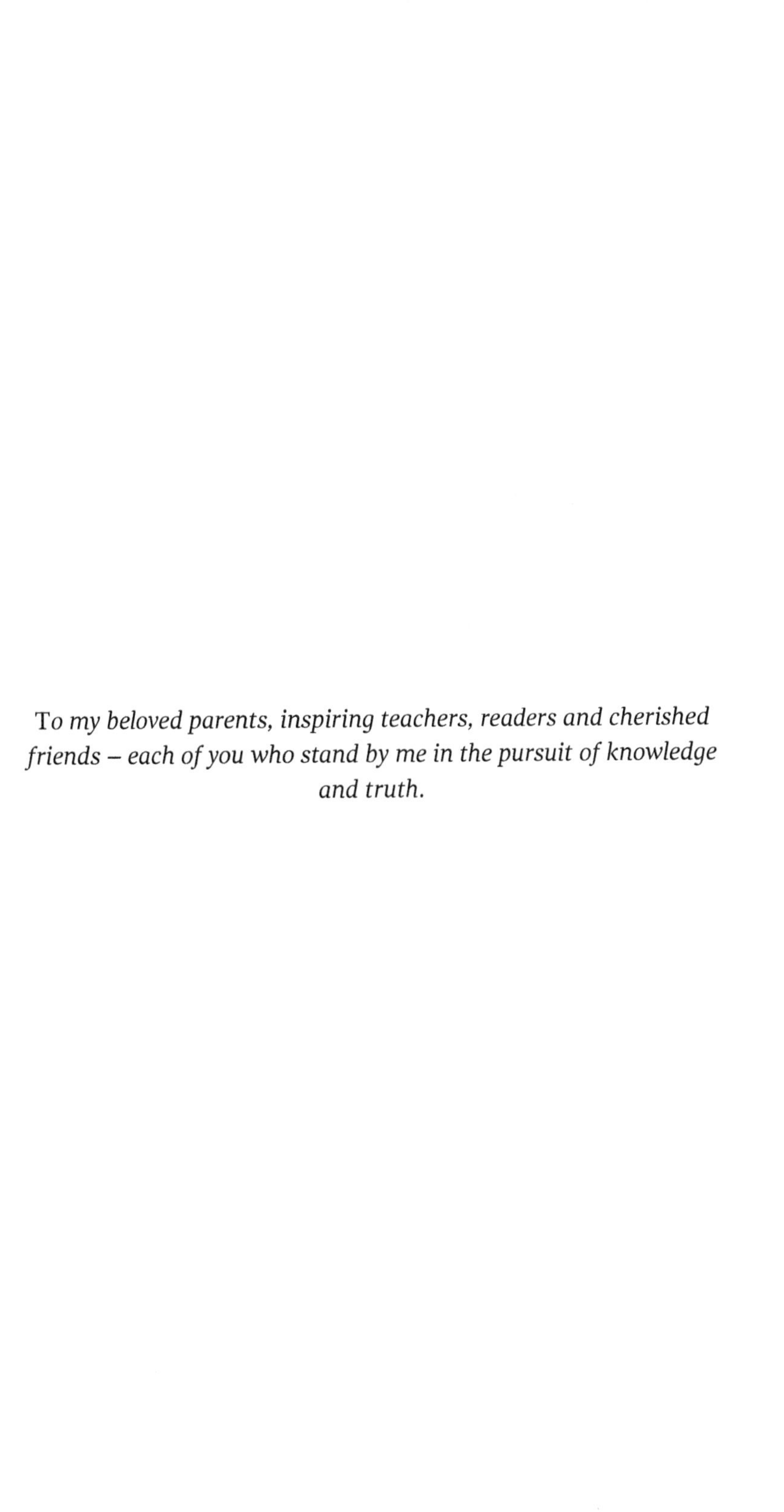

To my beloved parents, inspiring teachers, readers and cherished friends – each of you who stand by me in the pursuit of knowledge and truth.

Contents

Preface

Tablighi Jamaat, also called the Tablighi movement, provides one of the important instances of Islamic revival movements in the 2Ist Century. This movement emerged in the backdrop of conflicting and deteriorating conditions of the Muslims in the world, in particular India. After the demise of the global Islamic Caliphate existing till the early 20th century, the socio-political, economic conditions of the Muslims all over the world worsened. In India, the problem was more grievous. The condition of the Muslims during the later reign of the Mughal emperor became a pity. Oppression, corruption, irreligiosity and debauchery of Muslims became the order of the day. The *Ulama's* (scholars) and Islamic teachings were suppressed by Akbar. Instead, he advocated for multi-religious cultures and beliefs. Moreover, in British India, the Muslims were subjected to cultural onslaught both at the hands of the majority and rulers. The leaders and ideologies of the Hindu revivalist movements like Shuddi were advocating for forceful conversion of all Muslims of India whom they were merely looking as Hindu converts. Additionally, India, since the 17th century, was home to various Islamic revival movements. The great ideologies like Shah Waliullah, Ashraf Ali Thanvi, Sayid Ahmad Khan, Ahmad Raza Khan Barelvi, Mohamad Iqbal, Abul Ala Maududi and others played an important role in the religious reform and revival. All the above factors played a great role in the emergence and founding of Tablighi Jamaat by Maulana Ilyas Kandalwi with distinctive ideology and organisational structure.

Today Tablighi Jamaat is the most prominent and successful movement in the Islamic world. It would not be an exaggeration to say that this movement is present and affected the Muslims, wherever they live-Muslims. It is primarily due to its unique ideology and organizational structure, which are the core themes of this book. Thus the purpose of this study is to bring to light the unique features of the Tablighi movement with regard to its ideals, goals, techniques of work and organization in a simple, lucid and systematic way. All the available works both in Urdu and English were consulted for this work.

This book is the outcome of two chapters of my PhD research thesis entitled 'Two Faces of Islamic Movements in Kashmir Valley: A Comparative Study of Jamaat Islami and Tablighi Jamaat in Kashmir Valley' at Aligarh Muslim University. I hope this work will be valuable for academicians, researchers, scholars interested in Islamic movements in general and the Tablighi movement in particular. Moreover, this work will prove an asset to the sociology of religion and social movement literature. Additionally, I am sure that this book will also serve the need for a useful textbook in social movement theory, sociology of religion, especially in Islamic movement kinds of literature focusing on Tablighi Jamaat.

Rameez Ahmad

Acknowledgements

Alhamdulillah!

It is my privilege to express my sincere gratitude to my esteemed guide Prof. Syed. Zainuddin, Department of Sociology, Aligarh Muslim University, whose effective inspiration and endless encouragement realized the success of this work. My thanks and gratitude is to all the teachers, colleagues, research scholars of the department and friends for their valuable guidance and kind help..

My wholehearted gratitude goes to my parents, my family and my half of deen, who proved to be a great source of inspiration and moral support, and for their sincere dua's. I also thank my grandmother, 'Shahmaali', for her love and prayers, and; all my near's and dears for their support.

Above all, I humbly thank the Almighty Allah ("Subhaanahu wa ta'ala") for his endless blessings, which enabled me to complete my research work successfully despite numerous odds, from which the present book entitled 'Tablighi Jamaat: Ideology and Organisational Structure' was carved out. Without His help "my eye power, mental faculty and who keep me happy and healthy all the way," even a margin of this work would not have been possible. Thank you, my Rub, My Lord, the King, the sustainer and maintainer of the worlds and the universe.

August 23, 2021
Rameez Ahmad

Prologue

In the vast tapestry of Islamic history, certain movements emerge at pivotal moments to revive and reshape the faith, guiding communities through turbulent times. The Tablighi Jamaat, born in the early 20th century, is one such movement that has profoundly influenced Muslim societies worldwide. Founded by Maulana Ilyas Kandalwi, this movement arose during a time of intense socio-political upheaval, where Muslims faced challenges not only in maintaining their religious identity but also in countering external forces that sought to diminish their beliefs and practices.

In India, these challenges were amplified. Muslims found themselves grappling with the aftermath of colonial rule, socio-cultural pressures, and the rise of revivalist movements from other faiths. Amid this backdrop, the Tablighi Jamaat emerged as a beacon of hope, advocating a return to the fundamentals of Islam, emphasizing spiritual rejuvenation, and fostering a sense of brotherhood and unity.

This book aims to unravel the unique ideology, methods, and organizational structure that have made the Tablighi Jamaat a global phenomenon. It delves into the roots of the movement, the socio-political circumstances that facilitated its rise, and the profound impact it has had on the Islamic world.

As you turn these pages, you will embark on a journey through the Tablighi Jamaat's transformation—from a modest grassroots effort to one of the most influential Islamic movements of our time. This prologue serves as an invitation to explore a movement that continues to inspire millions, encouraging them to reconnect with their faith, nurture their spirituality, and uphold the principles of Islam in their daily lives.

Rameez Ahmad, September 30, 2024 (edition)

Abbreviations

TJ- TABLIGHI JAMAAT
PBUH- PEACE BE UPON HIM (PROPHET MOHAMMAD)
JI- JAMAAT ISLAMI
BJP- BHARTIA JANTA PARTY
AMU- ALIGARH MUSLIM UNIVERSITY

CHAPTER I

INTRODUCTION

Religious movements like 'Tablighi Jamaat' characterize one of the important aspects of social movements. In fact, there are some thinkers who have referred to 'religious' (Islamic movements) as 'inherently social movements,' though social movement theorists generally have excluded them from social movement literature, thinking it does not fit their categorizations. However, by integrating different categorizations, new theories of social movement literature could be used for explaining Islamic movements (Berna, 2008). In fact, religion has a much bearing on social movements, especially in the modern era. Social movements, mainly the religious since the foundation of sociology, have occupied the position of the cornerstone of the discipline. With the reinvigorated scholarly inquiry of 'New Religious Movements' especially after the 1980s, the sociology of religion too has opened promising approaches and re-conceptualizations to study religious movements. These view religious movements are primarily as a part of a more 'extensive world order' (Lechner, 1984; Wuthnow, 1980) Or 'globalization (Robertson, 1984; Robertson. R, 1989) and religious movements as a source of personal empowerment (Beckford, 1983; McGuire, 1983; John A. Hannigan, 1991).

Besides, in the era of globalization, especially since the 1970's Islam has proven to be a major force in the public life of Muslim Societies, confounding the presuppositions of a development theory predicated on the progressive westernization and secularization of society. In the decades following independence, most Muslim countries turned to their western allies for the development models. Across the Muslim world, many in their disillusionment began to reexamine and question their lot. Why were newly independent societies and governments impotent, authoritarian, poor, illiterate, and corrupt? Why, despite their western allies and western models of development, had so many Muslim countries remained weak and vulnerable? The experience of failure triggered criticism and a quest for identity and authenticity, as many decried their loss of not only political power but also cultural identity. The failure of increasingly discredited secular forms of nationalism, from Arab nationalism to Muslim nationalism, strengthened new voices who appealed to an Islamic alternative, calling for the Islamization or re-Islamization of society (Esposito, 1997; Delvoie and Esposito, 1998).

For almost four decades now, Islam has been reasserted as a source of political development and mobilization. The pervasive belief that nation-building required a clear secular orientation has been challenged in diverse ways across the Middle East, as well as in South, Southeast, and Central Asia. The role of Islam as a symbol of political legitimacy and a source of political and social activism and popular mobilization has become global in scope, as governments have appealed to Islam to enhance their legitimacy and authority, buttress nationalism, legitimate policies, and programs and increase popular support (Esposito, 1997; Delvoie and Esposito, 1998).

Modern Islamic social Movements and organizations have been the driving force behind the dynamic spread of the Islamic resurgence. They have also become a focal point or embodiment of an Islamic threat in the eyes of western governments as well as many governments in the Muslim world. For some, Islamic movements represent an authentic alternative to corrupt, exhausted, and ineffectual regimes. For many others, they are destabilizing forces- the tool of demagogues who will employ any tactic to gain power. The violence and terrorism perpetrated by groups with names like the party of God, Holy War, Army of God....conjure up images of irrational religious fanatics and a thirst for vengeance and a penchant for violence (Esposito, 1997; Delvoie and Esposito, 1998).

Yet, the reality is far more complex and diverse than its popular image. Alongside the violent radical rejectionists are Islamic organizations that espouse political liberalization and democratization. Since the late 1980s and early 1990s, in particular, Islamic organizations and Islamists have won seats in parliament, held portfolios' in cabinets, and emerged as the leading or a significant opposition in countries as diverse as Tunisia, Algeria, Egypt, Turkey, Lebanon, Jordan, Yemen, Kuwait, and Pakistan

The varieties of Islamic activist groups and experiences are a testimony to the flexibility of Islam, and political Islam in particular. They illustrate the extent to which specific contexts, differences of political economy, distinctive personalities and ambitions, individual leaders or ideologies, and Islam's capability of multiple and varied interpretations all shape the ideology and actions of the Islamic movements. This diversity underscores the multi meanings and usages of Islam and usages of Islam by Muslim rulers and Islamic organizations and their differing attitudes toward and relationships with the 'West' (Esposito, 1997; Delvoie and Esposito, 1998) or local regimes or the governments.

Thus, Islamic politics must be viewed within the specific country contexts because of far from a monolithic reality; it manifests a rich diversity of leaders, organizations, strategies, and tactics.

Moreover, the socio-political condition of the Muslims in India since the later period of the Mughal Emperor Akbar not only worsened, but irreligiosity, corruption, and debauchery became the order of the day. Under his new religion, *'Deen-i-Illahi'*[1] Akbar not only promoted ignorance and irreligiosity but also suppressed *'Ulama* [2]' (religious heads) and Islamic teachings. For instance, fire worship, interreligious marriages, prostration before court proceedings, banning of Prophet's name in Friday prayers, and false acclaim to be Prophet or Allah's incarnation. Then after the Aurangzeb and in British India, the political, religious, social, economic, educational, and cultural conditions of Muslims further deteriorated (Sabir, 2015). Thus various *'Ulama's'* and leaders like Shiekh Ahmad Sirhindi, Shah- Walluillah, Sir Syed Ahmad Khan, Allama Iqbal, Maulana Qasim Nanutavi, including the founder Tablighi Jamaat namely Maulana Mohamad Ilyas, came to reform the Muslim societies of such corruption and debauchery of the Muslims.

THEORETICAL BACKGROUND AND SIGNIFICANCE

As mentioned, since the inception of sociology, religious movements have occupied the position of the cornerstone of the discipline (John A. Hannigan, 1991). In fact, the very foundation of sociology has a religious bearing or 'stamp. The functional theorists of sociology like Parsons, Malinowski' especially 'Durkheim' saw religion as a basis of solidarity (Ritzer, 1996; Haralambos M and Heald R.M., 1997). Even Robert Bellah's concept of 'Civil Religion' or 'Americanism' in the 1960s held more or less the same view of Durkheim that in modern secular societies, it was the society worshipped and religion promoting cohesion (Bellah, Robert 1967).

Max Weber's interpretative sociology and 'phenomenological sociological approach' are also much relevant that they will enable us to understand the understandings and meanings which the members of Tableeghi Jamaat give to their actions (beliefs, values, behaviour, action, social relationships) within the ideology and organizational framework. Similarly, Conflict theorists like Karl Marx, George Simmel, Coser are of the view that conflict between groups enhances intragroup solidarity (Hall, 2003). The 'clash of the civilizations' thesis' of Huntington can also be placed within this 'conflict' perspective to study the said movement. In the case of Tableeghi Jamaat, this movement emerged in the wake of the conflicting-socio-politico environment of the world, in particular India. This movement was founded in the backdrop when Muslims were subjected to deterioration, biases, forced conversions, and cultural onslaught by Hindu fundamentalist movements (Ahmad, 2009).

Islam, for centuries, has shown extraordinary tendencies of mobilization of collective behaviour. Especially since 9/11, there has been great confusion and misunderstanding everywhere. Islam and the activities of Muslims are seen as a threat. They are labelled as terrorists, and Islam-o-phobia is on the rise. More often, discredited talks, objects, or images linked to Islam are drawing spectacular and tremendous global attention. Scholars and governments are puzzled over Islam's rallying, the potential of mass mobilization, or collective action. There is fear all around, and Muslims or Islamic movements are under great securitization (Esposito, 1997) as if all Muslims are terrorists. The Quran is burned, hijabs are torn, and the prophets are mocked and blasphemed. Muslims across the world, be it Afghanistan, Palestine, Syria, Iraq, Myanmar, Kashmir, Libya, China, India, or Pakistan, are subjected to brutal tortures, killings, rapes and are even bombed under the guise of tackling terrorism or fundamentalism. The very identity of Muslims or Islam is under great threat and confusion. Yet, one more reality to this end is that Muslims comprise about 23 per cent of the world population. So it is in this backdrop, understanding Islam or Islamic movements or their ideologies and activities are of utmost importance. The most promising 'theoretical tool' to understand 'Islamism' or Islamic movements is the 'Social Movement Framework.' This theory had its origin in the writings of social thinkers like Le Bon, Herbert Blumer, and William Kornhauser when they began inquiring about the nature of 'crowd behaviour' and movement. Modern-day 'social movement theory', especially from European social scientists, radically shift from 'mainstream materialism' and focus on newer 'value-based social movements, such as environmentalism, feminism, student movements, etc. Emanated from 'post-material or post-industrial politics, they suggest a new social constituency through both political and apolitical means or through formal (organized) or informal means. Social movement theories help in raising important questions like why and how the group behaves or acts in such a way? Why people or members of the group are politically active or inactive, either so collectively or individually? Or why do groups resist or bring about social change (Mamud, 2019)? 'Social Movement Theory' thus is an apt 'theoretical tool' to understand the working or ideology of Islamist movements like 'Tablighi Jamaat'.

METHODOLOGY

So far as my study is concerned, it's qualitative in nature. Within the 'qualitative research framework,' my study would be 'Basic Research' pure or fundamental research, aiming at generating knowledge; 'Descriptive Research' involving the description of the state of affairs of the movements; Analytical Research involving generating new generalizations by analyzing data or facts; and Exploratory Research, which helps in finding new facts. Nevertheless, Exploratory and Descriptive Researches are also categorized among the types of case studies (Tellis, 1997; Yin, 2004, IGNOU, n.d.-b). However, this work is mostly based on content analysis research methodology. Nevertheless, some part of the book is based on my case studies/interviews based on my field study of the Tablighi movement.

TABLIGHI JAMAAT

The word 'tabligh' is an Arabic originated word meaning 'to convey', 'to communicate', 'to preach' or to advise. The word 'Jamaat' is also Arabic originated word which means group, assembly, congregation or party. Thus Tablighi Jamaat can be simply translated as the preaching party. However, it must be noted that Maulana Ilyas, the founder of the TJ, never preferred his group to be called as a separate party. He has stressed that no one after the seal of prophethood ' could claim to form a new party. However, it appears that, Ilyas himself has preferred to call it 'Tahreek Emaan, meaning the movement of faith. Likewise, Haq (1972: 46) mentions;

"when Ilyas was asked to suggest a name for the movement, he is reported to have said that he was not founding any Jamaat; the Jamaat of the Muslims has already been formed-it has for its constitution the Quran, the mosque is the place of its activities, its centres are Mecca and Medina and in its programme are Hajj, Ramazaan and prayers. If he had to give a name to his work, he would call it Tahreek-i-Imaan."

Thus Ilyas's main aim of founding the movement appears to be refreshing the faith of the Muslims by making them strict followers of Islam by practising basic rituals or fundamentals of the Islam.

The foundation of the Tablighi Jamaat was laid down by Maulana Ilyas in the early 1920s. However, he formally launched it only in 1926, at Mewat, India. However, the inspiration to launch the movement and to devote his life to the preaching of Islam at the grassroots level through travel and by visiting door to door came to Ilyas during his second *Hajj* 'pilgrimage' to Hijaz-Mecca in 1926. According to one chronicler of the movement, the principles of the 'tabligh' preaching were conveyed to Ilyas by divine revelation in the course of his sojourn in Mecca. On his return to India, Ilyas started the practice of undertaking preaching tours and invited others to do likewise. His approach to preaching was quite humble. It is said in his early days; he used to cry, weep and plead before Mewatis to accept his preaching message even when being opposed (Agwani, 1986:41; Nadwi, n.d.; Sikand, 2002).

Tablighi Jamaat has emerged today as the most prominent transnational religious movement throughout the Muslim world. Its influence and success have been reported from North Africa, Pakistan, Bangladesh as well as among Muslim immigrants in the western European countries (like Germany, France, Switzerland), Eastern Europe (Denmark, UK), Canada and the United States and Australia. Moreover, its presence is found in about 150 to 200 countries. This is primarily because of its unique ideology and organizational features like its apolitical nature, focusing on touring, travelling or patrolling, showing aversion to publicity and perceiving dawah (preaching or invitation towards Islam) as the fundamental obligation of each and every Muslim enjoined by Allah, Prophet Mohammad(PBUH) or Quran (Lone 2021; Lone, 2018; Sikand, 2002; 2; Zainuddin 2020: 1).

'Tablighi Jamaat'isan ideological movement believing that it is the responsibility of each and every Muslim, not just *'ulama'* (scholars), to invite people towards Islam. They enjoin and interpret *'dawah'* (invitation) primarily in the light of two Quranic verses, that is, "let there arise out of you a band of people inviting to all that is good, enjoining what is right, and forbidding what is wrong" (Al 'Imran: 104), and "who is better in speech than one who calls (men) to Allah, works righteousness, and says, I am among the Muslims" (Quran, Fussilat: 33) (Masud, 2000). This 'enjoining the right and forbidding the wrong' is the responsibility and binding on each and every Muslim (as farz al-ayn: fundamental on each Muslim). Further, the Quranic verse which, reads as, 'O Messenger! Convey to others that which has been revealed unto you from your Lord' (Al-Ma'ida 5: 67) applies to every member of the Muslim Ummah (Troll. Christian W, 2019).

Unlike many Islamists who see 'dawah' as an 'Ulama' led project, 'Tablighi Jamaat' see it primarily an 'individual project' responsibility of each and every Muslim, including ordinary, illiterate and even handicapped[3]. They focus on the direct and oral methods of preaching and shun media and publicity. They view dawah or 'deen' not something to be read or talked about but as a practical activity, *'amaali kaam'*. Further, they advocate travel and tour methods of giving dawah directly to the Muslim masses all over the world. They are of the view that Prophets and the pious companions of the Muhammad (PBUH), also called 'Sahaba' did dawah in the same manner by travelling towards people. However, in 'Tablighi dawah project', unlike the Prophets and Sahaba, their focus is not on the conversion of Non-Muslims, but only on Muslims. They are of the opinion that it's quite illogical, irrational and merely a wastage of time to call Non-Muslims towards Islam when Muslims are not themselves truly practising Muslims. So their prime focus is on the Muslims only, "making them true self-conscious Muslims strictly abiding by the dictates of faith. This complete obedience to God Almighty Allah is also the condition for organizing politics successfully. In bestowing upon political authority and power, it is God —Allah's purpose that these believers protect and enforce His law and commandments on earth. If Muslims, first of all, are capable of accomplishing such obedience in the sphere acts of *'ibadat'* worship- how can they expect to be entrusted administration of the world and its peoples?

No wonder then that Ilyas, in the given circumstances, considered a political authority and power even undesirable given the present-day Muslims' negligence of God-Allah's laws in their personal lives, as he saw it. Hence totally aloof from politics - and that in the India of the 1930s, at the height of the struggle for independence and of the Muslim League's communal political appeal. Political discussion among the members of preaching groups is forbidden. As individuals, the workers are free to hold their own political and to participate in political affairs, provided they do not import these their religious endeavours or make use of their preaching activity furthering political ends (Khan, 1986; Sikand, 2002; Nadwi, n.d.). Moreover, TJ maintains a loose organizational structure by accommodating Muslims from diverse socio-political backgrounds in its faith renewal programme irrespective of the school of *fiqh* or thought.

Maulana Ilyas' Tablighi Jama'at inculcates the strict following of Muslim Personal Law, and it preaches the need to maintain the traditional details of Muslim lifestyle as to behaviour, personal demeanour, dress, including *'pardha'* (hijab and veils) for women, etc. In this respect, its thrust is not only conservative but revivalist as well. Hence, on the practical level, in a culturally and religious pluralist society like India, its impact entails stress on what makes Muslims different from others (Troll. Christian W, 2019).

As we know, context, that is, 'time, space, circumstances', play an important role in the foundation of an individual, group or any institution. These greatly affect the ideology, organization or behaviour of an individual or group. Usually, be it individuals or organizations, they are the products of time and space. The same is the case with Tablighi Jamaat. Broadly three external/social factors played an important role in the formation of Tableeghi Jamaat and shaping its ideology and organizational structure. The first was the threat of *irtidaad* 'apostasy' from Islam of the neo-Muslims in particular and of all Muslims in general due to their impracticality, weak *Emaan or* faith in Islam. Thus Ilyas tried to make such Muslims true and strictly practising Muslims. This threat was posed by Shuddhi and Sangthan 'Hindu revivalist movements and partly by Christian missionary efforts in the late 19th and early 20th centuries. Ilyas thus started his project of *tabligh* invitation among the Meows of Mewat (neo-Muslims), who were still practising their age-old Hindu customs and thus were the soft targets of these Hindu and Christian revivalist projects. Thus TJ came as a reaction against the Arya Samaaj (Shuddhi and Sangathan) movements and the Christian missionary efforts, which led the Muslim community and scholars to organize their own preaching and missionary movements.

Second, Muslims throughout the world were subjected to a decline in political power and consequently religious power. There was a state of mess, disorder, corruption and uneasiness among the Muslims in particular after the demise of the global Islamic Caliphate. The Muslim reformers and intellectuals were much concerned with the abject condition of the Ummah. There was a strong zeal among many Muslims to revive the Caliphate system. In this backdrop, in 1919, the Khilafat movement was also launched in India to restore Ottoman Caliphate. In the meantime, Muslims were subjected to many conflicts and oppression throughout the world. In India, too, by the 1900s the Hindu -Muslim conflict had become endemic, where elites of both the communities were fiercely competing for the colonial patronage. The Mapilla Revolt of 1921 by the poor peasant community against the high caste Hindus and Bristish further complicated the problem. Thereafter the Hindu revivalist movements doubled the efforts of conversion of Muslims to Hindu fold by hook or crook (Sikand, 2000). Thus these deteriorating and conflicting socio-political conditions were reflected differently by different Muslim intellectuals and socio-religious reformers. Tableeghi Project could be termed as the response or reflection of the Maulana Ilyas to such conflicting and abject circumstances of the Muslims.

Third, TJ was the byproduct of the medieval Sufism (which focused on Quran and injunctions of Shariah, unlike popular Sufism) and Muslim missionary activism in India, which focused on tolerance, equality, piety, instruction, guidance, true Islam in a caste-ridden society, unlike Hinduism or early Christian missionaries which focused stratification, inequality and to prove their superiority over other religions respectively.

Ilyas himself belonged to the Sabriyah branch of the Chastiyah order, which is non-mystical (Gabario, 2006), focusing much on Quran, Sunnah and Shariah. He strictly opposed music and sima [4], unlike mainstream Chastiyah order and also opposed tomb worship, grave worship, gathering of men and women at such places, prostrating there and unveiled women. Thus he was against anything opposed to Shariah. However, like Chastiyah order, he showed aversion to political affairs and, consequently under its influence, divorced religion from politics. Ilyas considered himself as the successor of Shah Walli-u-llah in the internal caliphate to teach the Muslims fundamentals of their religion (Haq, 1972). Thus Ilyas's immediate focus was on the internalization of Shariah or caliphate before Muslims could preach about the externalization of Shariah in a non-conducive environment of a conflicting socio-political world. Moreover, during the same time, many great Islamic thinkers like Maulana Asraf Ali Thanvi (1863-1943), Khawaja Hassan Nizami (1878-1955), Maulana Abdul Bari (1878-1926), Syed Abu Ala Maududi(1903-79) etc. called upon all Muslims, *Ulamas* (religious scholars), Sofi's to fight against *irtidaad* (*Shuddi* campaign) by safeguarding their religion through *tabligh* (preaching or invitation). All these missionary activisms on the part of Muslim Scholars also affected the faith movement of the Maulana Ilyas. The ideology and organizational structure of the movement has been discussed in the following chapters.

The present study is divided into four chapters. The first chapter, entitled '**Introduction**', deals briefly with the status of Islamic resurgence, theoretical background, methodology....... Moreover, I have also discussed how the social movements, primarily religious, characterize the important aspect of 'sociology of religion or sociology. In the next sub-theme, 'theoretical background,' I have discussed various theories of sociology (like functionalist, conflict, interactionist, phenomenological, etc.) concerning my study. The collective behaviour theory, resource mobilization theory, and in particular, 'social movement theory' have also been examined in the present study. This chapter also includes a brief introduction about the TJ.

The second chapter, entitled **'Tablighi Jamaat: Ideology'**, deals with the 'Ideology' of the Tablighi movement. In this chapter, I have discussed the socio-political landscape, which helped in the emergence of the movement and which conditioned its ideology. This is followed by a full-length discussion of the ideology of the movement, including its various characteristics in a systematic way. The six principles of the Tablighi Jamaat *'chai batien'*, which constitute the important portion of its ideology, have also been discussed in this chapter. The six principles are then followed by the 'translation of Maulana Saad's Speech' and its brief 'summary' about its relevance with the ideology of the Tablighi Jamaat. The third chapter, **'Tablighi Jamaat: Organizational Structure'**, deals with the organizational structure of the Tablighi Jamaat. It brings about various organizational strategies of the group and how its members carry and organize their work from mosques *'masjids'* and at various levels of headquarters through touring, travelling, patrolling, and meeting the people. The organizational structure at various levels like global, state, and district levels have also been discussed in this chapter. Furthermore, this chapter contains various organizational strategies of the TJ and three case studies based on my interview with TJ members. In addition to the above, the recent split in the organizational structure has also been briefly dealt with.

The fourth chapter, entitled **'Conclusion and Summary'**, is an outline of the whole book. The main points of the book 'ideology and organizational structure of the TJ' have been summarized. The status of the movements during Covid-19 has also been briefly dealt with in this concluding chapter.

Footnotes

[1]. Deen-i-Illahi or din-e-Illahi, literally meaning 'religion of God' was founded by Mughal Emperor in 1582. It was a 'belief system' based on mixture of various beliefs or religions.

[2]. Ulama meaning learned men or religious scholars.

[3]. As revealed by Tableeghi Jamaat members in the interview and saw personally few blind members in the group busy in Tablighi activities and preaching.

[4]. Listening to music, singing, chanting and measured recitation in order to produce religious emotion and ecstasy through ones voice or by musical instruments.

CHAPTER II

TABLIGHI JAMAAT: IDEOLOGY

The socio-political conditions around the world, and in particular, British India, not only helped in the emergence of the Tablighi Jamaat but also shaped and conditioned the ideology of the movement. The end of the Turkish caliphate, together with the declining political powers of the Muslims into the hands of the British, hurt the sentiments of the Muslims all over the world, including India. This is also reflected in the ideas and teachings of the Maulana Mohammad Ilyas. Looking at the world around him, Ilyas came to believe that the fall of the Muslims from the heights of power and prosperity was actually Allah's punishment for their having strayed from the path of Islam and for having given up their responsibility of constantly engaging in *tabligh* (preaching or invitation), having wrongly left this task to the *Ulama* alone. The Muslim *Ummah* [5] (worldwide Muslim community) could he repeatedly stressed, regain its lost glory- Caliphate of Allah on earth only if every Muslim began to lead his or her life strictly according to the dictates of Islam and constantly engage in its *da'wah* [6] (invitation) and *tabligh* (Numani, n.d.). It was the religious duty of each Muslim to see himself or herself foremost as *muballig* [7] or missionary of Islam. God Ilyas said had promised the Muslims that if they faithfully followed the path of the Prophet Muhammad (PBUH) and devoted themselves to the task of Islam, they would always dominate over non-believers and would be destined to be the masters of each and everything on this earth (Kandhalawi, 1989: 8). Meanwhile, the serious threat posed by the *Shuddi* [8] (Arya Samaj) and Sangathan-Hindu revivalist movements to the very survival and identity of Muslims in colonial India also shaped and conditioned the ideology of the Jamaat. Arya efforts of *Shuddhi* (purification) among neo-Muslim groups as well as their virulent attacks on Islam-all part of a larger elite Hindu project of constructing a homogeneous Hindu community identity pitted sharply against the Muslims. Moreover, other seems to have played no small role in the steady worsening of inter-communal relations in larger parts of northern India. By the 1900s, Hindu- Muslim conflict had become endemic, with community elites fiercely competing with each other for the crumbs of colonial patronage. A brief lull in communal conflict seems to have set in. However, with the signing of the Lucknow Pact in 1916 and the launching of the Khilafat agitation in 1919 to restore the Ottoman caliphate in the course of which Hindu and Muslim leaders agreed to work with each other in a common struggle against the British (Minault, 1982). What was particularly significant in the course of the Khilafat movement was the rapid growth and spread of pan-Islamic sentiments throughout the country, thus building upon the earlier efforts to generate a pan-Indian Muslim community identity. As Minualt demonstrates, the Khilafat itself assumed the form of powerful symbol around which the construction and crystallization of an India wide Muslim community were sought to be further strengthened. The agitation for restoring the Turkish caliphate actually helped further consolidate the sense of distinct Indian Muslim community. It also enabled the *'Ulama'* (scholars) to establish links with ordinary Muslims all over the country, seeking to rally them under their leadership for the pan-Islamic cause.

The blow to the brief Hindu-Muslim honeymoon was not long on coming. In August 1921, fired by the anti-British and pan Islamic zeal spread by the Khilafatists, the Mapilas of Malabar, an impoverished Muslim peasant community living in the deep south of India, rose up in a violent revolt against the British authorities and their local allies, the landlords, almost all of whom happened to be high caste Hindus. Thus communal tensions and violence between Hindus and Muslims, which during the course of the khilafat and non-cooperation movements, had declined significantly, suddenly reached new and unprecedented heights all over India, especially in the north. However, it is here noteworthy to mention that efforts of Shuddi conversion, especially of Malkans

(Nau-Muslims) [9]) of the western districts of United provinces who were claiming to be descendants of Jaduan Rajputs, though some of them also possessed Jat, Agarwal, Bania, and Tarkar Brahmin ancestry (Hasan, 1997: 210), had started in the 1900s when Arya Shuuddhi Subhas was set at various places in Malkana belt by Pandit Bhoj Raj Sharma. By 1910, the Rajput Shuddi Sabha, which along with the Arya Samaj, was actively engaged in the *Shuddi* campaign, claimed to have brought some 1052 Malkanas into the Hindu fold (Jones, 1972:131). But, following the events in Malabar in 1921, which galvanized the Aryans into reviving *Shuddhi* campaign, missionary efforts now began to be taken up on a war footing by activists of the Arya Samaj and the Rajput Shuddhi Sabhas in the Malkana belt. Within the first few months of 1922, over 5000, Malkanas are said to have undergone *Shuddhi,* and the figure rose up to 30,000 by the end of the year (Hasan, 1997:210). After Malkanas, the Aryas and the Sanatanis now began to extend their conversion to other nau-Muslims (neo-Muslims) groups. Work in this direction was started among the Muslim Jats and Gujjars of Punjab and the western districts of the United Provinces, and these efforts seem to have met with some success. Appeals were then issued to target virtually all the Muslims of India for *Shuddhi.* At a public rally at Lahore, Shraddhanand, in a fiery speech, exhorted the Hindus to bring back to Hinduism 65 million Indian Muslims (Sikand, 2000). Branding Islam as a bloodthirsty religion bent on exterminating all unbelievers, Muslims, he declared, had launched a jihad against the Hindus (Shraddhanand, 1925).

So looking at the conflicting socio-political conditions around the world and in particular, India, where Islamic identity and in particular neo-Muslims were under threat of Hindu revivalist movements, Ilyas started his project of 'da'wah' among the nau-Muslims of Mewat who were still retaining many of their age-old customs and traditions, linked with Hinduism (Numani, 1989:21). It is here that he devised the ideology of the 'Jamaat', focusing on making Muslims good Muslims and not on the conversion of non-

Muslims. So the immediate focus of the Tablighi project was not so much the conversion of non-Muslims to Islam as making Muslims 'true', self-conscious Muslims, strictly abiding by the dictates of their faith. Ilyas maintained that it was better for the Muslims to follow their faith strictly before they go out to invite non-Muslims to Islam. By doing so, non-Muslims would be thus impressed to see the Muslims practising Islam according to the dictates of 'Shariah.' Similarly, Mumtaz Ahmad (ed. 1994) argues, "the message of the Tableeghi Jamaat is simple, 'aey Muselmanu, Muselmaan banno" (oh you Muslims, be good – truly practising Muslims). Likewise, I.S Marwa in his article, "Tabligh Movement Among the Meows of Mewat", (Marwah, 1979: 96-97), writes, " the exclusive focus of Tablighi Jamaat was not the conversion of Muslims but making Muslims pure and better Muslims strictly abiding the Islamic code of conduct." Besides focusing only on the Muslims, in its 'da'wah' project, the main idea and foremost concern before Ilyas or Tablighi Jamaat was the idea to secure and save all the neo-Muslims who were under threat of Hindu Conversion movements and were still practising their old Christian or Hindu customs or traditions. So the central idea was to purify these nau-Muslims of their previous customs and traditions, having nothing to do with Islam. Thus Mumtaz Ahmad (Ahmad, 1991) writes, "a Muslim missionary movement, namely the Tablighi movement of Maulana Mohamad Ilyas came as a response against the militant Hindu movements of Shuddhi and Sangathan, need to be seen in the proximate context. The important thrust before the Tableeghi Jamaat was to purify these borderline Muslims of their previous Hindu accretions and to educate them about Islamic beliefs and rituals so that they could not easily fell in the net of these Hindu conversion movements". Ilyas principle aim then was the spread of Islamic teachings among all Muslims as cited above and in particular among ordinary Muslims. Given the backdrop of the menacing *iritidad* (apostasy) onslaught of the Aryas, Ilyas believed that the strongest defense against the threat of the apostasy was the spread of basic Islamic teachings among the Muslim masses. He believed that it was the duty of all Muslims, both men as well as women, to have a minimum knowledge of Islam necessary for them to carry out their religious ritual obligations (*fara'iz*). There was no need; however, he felt, for every Muslim to become an 'alim, and in matters related to the intricacies of Islamic law, ordinary Muslims could always resort to their own 'ulama for instruction (S. A. Khan, n.d.,: 27). Likewise, M.S. Agwani (Agwani 1986:40), writes 'it is the duty of each and every Muslim to invite others to Islam or to create Islamic awareness among other people, and one does not need necessary to be a religious scholar or 'alim for that.' Besides, in the Quranic commandment of 'command what is good and forbid what is evil' (Quran 3: 104, 110), Ilyas saw a divine order to all Muslims, and not just a selected few such as the 'ulama or the Sufis, to engage in the work of the *tabligh*. This responsibility, which has been bestowed by God-Allah upon all the prophets, had, after Muhammad's death, been entrusted to the entire Muslim Ummah. One did not have to be 'aalim (scholar) to be a *mubbaligh* (preacher). Indeed, one did not have to fully practice Islam or even all of what one preached before setting out to engage in *tabligh*, among others. Allah, it was said, would himself guide one to the path of good deeds simultaneously with one's own participation in the work of the Tableeghi Jamaat (Kandhalawi, 1989) n.d.:18-19). For Ilyas, every Muslim was striving to embody Islam within himself, taking the companions of Muhammad (PBUH) as his mode in order to achieve salvation. This call for each individual Muslim to constantly and consciously strive towards emulating the companions in his own personal life represented a radical break from traditional South Asian Muslim modes of piety, in which the intercession of a whole hierarchy of saints was seen as the key to ensuring one's entry into paradise as well as fulfilling one's own worldly desires (Sikand, 2002: 68).

The importance that Ilyas gave to the role of ordinary believers in his project of Islamization did not mean bypassing the 'ulama. Rather, the 'ulama were to have their own special place in his scheme of things. They were to have themselves step out from their madaris and, like the companions of the Prophet, go from house to house, exhorting people to participate in Tablighi project (Falahi, 1996:305). In fact, he saw 'ulama (the learned), as the allies of his da'wah project and maintained that if the learned will not join him, his movement will remain un-completed or unaccomplished. In other words, his movement will not benefit much unless 'ulama join his faith movement, and their cooperation was a must for the success of his efforts. He wrote to Maulana Zakariya, "for a long time it has been my opinion that until the learned themselves go and knock on the doors of the masses and tour villages and towns like common folk, my work will not reach a measure of completion because the action of the learned will have on the masses cannot be accomplished by their fiery speeches" Worried by the growing distance between the 'ulama and common Muslims, Ilyas repeatedly stressed that he wanted to bring the two groups closer together and to strengthen the control of the 'ulama as leaders of the masses who, in his view, were gradually falling prey to 'un-Islamic' ways and beliefs (Haq, 1972:95). He regarded the growing gulf between 'ulama and ordinary Muslims as 'most unfortunate for the community, and a grave danger for the future of Islam, because it foreshadowed apostasy and irreligiousness (ibid.,: 4) At a speech before an audience of 'ulama, one of Ilyas's leading disciple, Sayyid Abul Hasan Ali Nadwi, declared that if the 'ulama did not strengthen their relations with the community by participating in the work of Tablighi Movement, they would 'become an untouchable minority' to whose culture and way of life of common Muslims 'would become total strangers'.'Even their language and ideas, he warned it would be unfamiliar to the general public, necessitating a translator between the two' (Haq, 1972:133).

Thus the central thrust of Ilyas's Tablighi Project was the one it placed on each individual Muslim to uphold, to embody the basic tenets of Islam. The 'Shariah' mindedness was to focus in particular on exhorting Muslims to emulate the lives of the companions of Mohammad down to every small detail. In a context where Muslim political power was no more, each Muslim man and woman was now charged with the responsibility of upholding the 'Shariah'. They were to bring Islam firstly and above all into their personal lives, not in matters of just ritual devotion but also in their own behaviour and deportment. The focus then was on the transforming of the individuals as a means to gradual Islamisation of social institutions and structures, a process that would conclude only in the definite future. Since it was the individual Muslim who was the focus of the attention of the Tablighi project, particular importance was placed on the symbolic value of the physical body as a repository or reflection of Islamic commitment, as a site of crucial makers of identity clearly setting apart Muslims fromothers. Thus Islamic dress was seen inseparable from one's own commitment to the practice of Islam. Tablighi activists were expected to make a public announcement of their commitment to Islam by wearing a modest dress such as that worn by Prophet. Over time, in fact, there developed a sort of Tablighi uniform, which, while not compulsory enforced, was invariably strictly adhered to by activists while in Jamaat and even after-long, loose-fitting garments that ended just above the ankles, with prayer caps and turbans as head-dress. Another distinguishing bodily symbol on which particular importance was placed was facial hairs for males. Men were to shave their moustaches and keep their beards (at least one fistful long). This was, after all, Sunnat of the Prophet Muhammad himself, who it was said, had enjoined upon his followers to clearly distinguish them from the non-believers, for, as the hadith [10] had testified, if a person practised the customs of another community, God would raise him among them on the day of judgment (Nasr, 1994). Such external makers of identity, wrote Maulana Zakriya, were so important that their protection is thought to be the protection of one's own community and religion. Indeed, he maintained one should be even ready to lay down one's life to protect these symbols that mark off the slaves of God from those who rebel against Him (Zakkriyya, n.d.,:19).

Simultaneously, with the cultivation of their faith and improving their knowledge and practice of the basic ritual observances and the six principles [11] in the course of the jamaat activities were expected to engage in *tabligh* activity among the Muslims in the areas they visited. This, however, was considered secondary to self-improvement (Alam, 1985). Activists were simply to present the message of Islam before others, for that was what the Prophet himself had been commanded to do by God. Accordingly, activists were first to perform *gasht* or to patrol in the localities where Muslims lived, knocking on people's doors, inviting the male members of the families to join them in offering the evening- *Isha* prayers in the local mosque. During ghast, they were to be accompanied by wealthy or influential local men, to put at ease any apprehension that the people they addressed might have. After *Isha*, the congregation would be asked to stay on to listen the '*bayaan*' (lecture), which was delivered by a speaker from among the muballighin. In his '*bayaan [12]*' lecture, the speaker would passionately appeal to those present in the congregation to strengthen their faith, to regularly practice the obligatory rituals, and also to spare time-from just a day to several months, depending on their own convenience- to join a roving jamaat. They would be told all about the great rewards that they would earn for this as laid down in the books of faza'il (Sikand, 2002:78).

Although great importance was given to going out of one's home on Jamaat, Ilyas stressed that the actual sphere for the activist was his own locality and family (Ferozepuri, n.d.-a). After he returned from the jamaat, he was expected to continuously engage in Tablighi efforts among his family and neighbours, exhorting them to strengthen their faith, abide in their personal lives by the laws of the 'Shariah' and also to participate in the work of the jamaats. He was to regularly perform their '*gasht*' in his locality and arrange for daily *taleem [13]* session in his own home, where portions of the Faza'il 'Amal, the Quran, and the books of the traditions would be read out to members of the family (M. R. Qasmi, n.d.). He was also expected to encourage the women of his family to go out on the jamaat though the rules for women's jamaats were different from those meant for men. They were expected to play an important role in the work of the Tabligh, for this responsibility rested with all the believers. Although, in essence, women's Tablighi work is similar to that of women, special rules are to be followed when women go out in the Jamaat. They must be accompanied by their husbands or any other such close male relative; they must observe strict purdah [14], and special lodging facilities must be made for them. Their principal work, however, lies in their homes, which they are expected to organize daily *ta'lim* sessions for their families, in which portions form the Faza'il 'Amal is readout. The number of women actively involved in Tabligh's work is small, and most women involved in Tablighi activities are wives of men who are themselves active in the movement (Sikand, 1999: 41-52).

Ghast (patrolling) approach and ideology of 'da'wah' came as a reaction against his disappointing experience of *Madrassa* education or religious schools. He viewed that these *Madrassa's* (religious schools) were merely producing religious functionaries and not preachers (Ahmad, 1991). Gradually, thus Ilyas became dissatisfied with the work undertaken on an individual basis in these *Madrassa's* (schools). He felt that these *Madrassa's* (schools) were not free from the influence of the irreligious environment in which they functioned. First, it was not possible to impart complete training to all the children; secondly, the pupils who had been trained in these schools were soon 'drowned in the absolutely dark ocean of ignorance and irreligiousness around them' (S. A. H. A. Nadwi, n.d.); thirdly, the parents who had to be coaxed into sending their children into school could not appreciate or respect the knowledge thus acquired. As a result, the schools had no influence on the lives of the parents (Haq, 1972: 108). Besides, the same author writes, 'Ilyas felt that when engrossed in their daily chores, the poor Mewati cultivators had very little time or opportunity to learn about Islam. He could not insist that they become pupils in the *Maktab* (elementary school) or Madrassa (middle/upper school) at their age. Mere exhortation and advice would not revolutionize their lives and make them tread the Islamic path. Ilyas felt the only way for Mewati's was to go in groups and spend some time in centres of religious learning, observing the lives and actions of the learned and the pious, listening to their discourses on the life of the Prophet Mohammad (PBUH), his companions, and other religious matters and also learning to read the Quran (ibid., 111). Anwarul Haq (Haq, 1972:110) and Yoginder Sikand (Sikand, 2002:140) write that on August 2, 1934, at Nuh [15], Ilyas addressed Meow leaders to pledge that they will strictly abide and spread the 'basic principles of Islam, hold panchayat's to carry out the work of *tabligh* or religious renewal and will never give up this work of '*tabligh*' at any time in their life. Besides, he advised them to follow fifteen points' strictly, which are as follows:

(i) The Kalima or Article of Faith. (ii). Prayers (iii) Acquisition and dissemination of religious knowledge. (iv) Observing Islamic appearance or dress. (v) Observing Islamic ceremonies and rejecting non-Islamic ones. (vi) Performing nikah and marriage ceremony in the Islamic manner. (vii) Seclusion of women. (viii) Adherence to Islamic dress by women. (ix) Strict observance of Islamic beliefs and rejection of other religions or un-Islamic beliefs. (x) safeguarding and perseverance of mutual rights. (xi) Participation of learning, responsible and respectable person in every meeting or convention. (xii) Not to impart secular education to children before religious learning. (xiii) Pledge to strive and endeavour for the preaching of religion. (xiv) Observance of cleanliness and (xv) Pledge to shield the honour, dignity, and respect of one another or common Muslims.

However, Ilyas felt that if people did not diligently make this program of struggle for religion an integral part of their lives, their condition would deteriorate and would become worse than it was before. In his letter to Miya Muhamad 'Isa, Ilya wrote about the new way of 'da'wah' or preaching called 'ghast' or preaching tours from area to area or house to house 'unless you people are very diligent about making preaching tours part of your lives and go from one area to another for four months, you will not be able to enjoy the fruits of true religiousness and belief. Whatever you have achieved is temporary. If the endeavour is given up, you will be degraded further. Until now, it was your ignorance shielding you, and people did not notice you. Now, unless you protect yourselves with the strengthening of religious beliefs, you will fall victim to other peoples or your enemies (S. A. H. A. Nadwi, n.d.). To make 'da'wah' an everlasting activity, Ilyas demanded the following principles for Muslims generally and in particularly Mewatis (or preaching parties) to follow apart from six principles, strictly viz. that;

(i) Every week that they should preach in their own locality about the basic principles of religion (kalima and ritual prayers); forming a regular group under a leader and adopting the proper method to tour their neighbourhood;

(ii) For three days every month, they should go to nearby villages within a distance of five kilometres or miles (which the Mewatis used to call panch Kosa) to preach and hold meetings to persuade the local people to undertake similar tours; and,

(iii) For at least four months (three chillah's) they should leave their home and go to centres of learning to study about religion (Haq, 1972: 116).

Besides calling for strict adherence to 15 points and few principles, as mentioned above, he advocated daie's (those who call towards Islam) involved in the renewal of faith of their ignorant brothers in Islam, to observe utter humbleness while in da'wah or preaching. It is said that Ilyas's call, in the beginning, was heavily resisted. At a number of places, he was stoned, chased out with sticks from many villages. Yet, he did not surrender for the moment. He instead accepted his maltreatment happily at the hands of the people and thanked the Almighty Allah that he met the same resistance; the way prophets had undergone the trials, tribulations and tests in the way of Allah for the sake of Allah in spreading the message of Islam [16](Mazhari, 1972).

The preachers involved in the faith renewal were attempting to win their opponents in a very delicate and humble way. They were begging before the ones not coming to the mosque in a way that they even were removing their turbans and placing them at their feet, requesting them that they must come to the mosques. Thus people who were not interested in deen or offering prayers and coming to the mosque were won with utter humbleness and great humility. This is how the work of the 'tabligh' or 'faith movement' of Maulana Ilyas began[17] (Baliyavi, n.d.).

Ilyas subscribed to what is commonly called the Deobandi school of thought, and it was the teaching of the founding 'ulama of this school that he sought to popularize. These 'ulama had, in 1867, come together to set up a large madrasa, the Dar-ul 'Uloom, at Deoband, a town in northern India not far from Delhi (for details see (Metcalf, 1982); (Singhanawi, n.d.).They saw themselves as bringing back to life the days of the companions of the Prophet through their writings and speeches and issuing of legal opinions or fatwa (Usmani, 1995:3). They were strict adherents of Hanafi Islamic law and saw themselves as guardians of the shari'ah and crusaders against popular religious practices and beliefs among the Muslims which they believed contravened the Shariat. In this, they claimed to be carrying on in the reformist tradition of the renowned 'alim of the eighteenth-century Dehli, Shah Walilullah (1703-62), his son, Shah AbdulAziz (1746-1824) and his follower and leader of a militant jehad movement, Sayyed Ahmad Barelwi (1786-1831). Of particular concern to them were the threats posed by westernization, Christianity, secularization and materialism and the consequent laxity on the part of the many Muslims in matters of religious observance and their growing alienation from the 'ulama. Besides, above his ideology and movement, he was also influenced by many great Islamic thinkers and contemporaries of his time like Maulana Ashraf Ali Thanvi (1863-1943), Maulana Abdul Bari (1878-1926), Khawaja Hassen Nizami (1878-1955) and Abul Ala Maududi (1903-79). The great Deobandi 'alim, and spiritual preceptor of Ilyas, Maulana Ashraf Ali Thanvi, is said to have undertaken several Tablighi tours of the Shuddhi affected areas. In 1924, he prepared an elaborate program of *tabligh* to counter the Shuddhi challenge. This program which he called 'Tahfim-al Muslims', sought to spread basic Islamic knowledge among the Nau-

Muslims (Masud, 2000). Through numerous tracts and books, Thanvi sought to rouse the Muslims to effectively counter the Aariya *iritidad* campaign (Z. M. Nadwi, n.d.). He gave central importance to the assertion that the Quran and Sunnah- Prophetic traditions require every Muslim, and not just the 'ulama or Sufis, to engage in the work of the *tabligh*, for the command to 'enjoin what is good and forbid what is evil' is binding on all believers. In Gods eyes, nothing is more pleasing than *tabligh*. Tabligh, or the Islah (reform) of others, is obligatory(farz) for all Muslims, just as prayers, fasting, hajj are, and without it salvation is impossible. Here Thanvi, like Ilyas after him, calls for ordinary Muslims to restrict themselves to tabligh of the basic aqa'id (beliefs) alone. They must, he says, leave the often contentious domain of the masa'il (matters of the detailed application of the law) to the 'ulama, who, however, are warned not to focus while preaching on issues on which different schools of Islamic law are divided (ibid.).

The aim of *tabligh* (preaching or invitation towards Islam), says Thanvi, is to make Muslims follow more strictly the sunnah of the prophet. Here a careful distinction must be made between the Sunnat related to the Prophet's personal habits (*sunnat-i-'adat*) and that related to his worship (*sunnat-i-'ibadat*), only the latter being obligatory. Tablighi activists, in other words, should not be particularly rigid in enforcing the sunnat-i-'adat of Muhammad as that will make their mission even more difficult (Z. M. Nadwi, n.d., 325-27). Thanvi advises them to follow a pragmatic approach by not insisting that the 'Shariah' be strictly followed all the once, for this might prove to be seriously counterproductive. Thus, he says, if a person were to agree to become a Muslim only on the condition that prayer would not be made obligatory for him, his proposal should be accepted, for a while he refuses to pray, to begin with, he would himself start doing so when his faith in Islam begins to deepen after his conversion to Islam (ibid.: 195). This is one of the main ethics in the Tablighi ideology, which we listen to and learn in Tablighi circles and congregation and while they preach in local gatherings or give 'da'wah' to Muslims and non-Muslims. Similarly, if in a certain case a bid'a turns out to be the only 'source of the protection of Islam', then it, in that case, should be considered not just lawful, but in fact, obligatory (ibid.: 233). If recourse to bid'ah (innovation in Islam) were the only way that this could be done, then it should actually be considered a blessing rather than a curse (ibid.: 122-23).

Similarly, Khawaja Hassan Nizami, a prolific writer having amazing 500 books to his credit, in the wake of the *Shuddhi* campaign, penned a number of handbills, posters, and pamphlets and distributed them through the Halqa-i-Masha'ikh, a body of Sufi divines, to warn Muslims of the Arya threat (Naqvi, 1978: 149). Besides, he is said to have undertaken several missionary tours to outlying rural areas inhabited by Nau- Muslim communities. Of Nizami's several writings on Tableegh as a response to *shuddhi,* his Dai-i Islam (The Missionary of Islam) is the most prominent (K. H. Nizami, 1923). Maulana Maududi, at the height of the Malkana *irtidad* also wrote some treatises and books like Islam ka Sarchasma-i-Quvvat (The Source of Islam's Power) about *tabligh* in the 1920s. Islam or invitation towards it is not only limited to the verbal or written appeal. 'The whole life of the Prophet and his companions', writes Maududi, was a manifestation of the invitation to the truth. This included every action of theirs, in both the private as well as in public spheres. Moreover, it was not simply a small group among the early Muslims who have engaged in the *tabligh* "da'wah' ' of Islam. Rather, every Individual Muslim acted as a missionary (Maududi, 1988: 8-9). Both Islam and the fundamental aim of Muslim life are one and the same- 'inviting people to truth'. Tabligh then is Islam's real source of power' (ibid. 6-8). Besides individual Tablighi workers at the local level, the 'ulama and Sufis, too, have a crucial role to play in the vast, community-wide project of *tabligh.* If they fail in this, there is no way they can escape severe divine punishment that is certain to be visited upon them (ibid. 62-63). Maulana Abdul Bari, the renowned scholar and the politician of Firangi Mahal Madrasa of Lucknow, also played a major role in galvanizing Muslim public opinion in favour of the massive *tabligh* campaign. He argued that roving mendicants should form groups and travel to nau-Muslim villages. There they should spend a part of the day working as labourers, and in the evenings, should gather the people to teach them, Islam. They should earn their daily bread through their own labour. The Sufis and the Ulama should organize small groups comprising of at least three people, including one with a knowledge of medicine, another experienced in worldly matters, and the third, reasonably well versed in Islam. These groups should be dispatched to the villages inhabited by the Nau-Muslims, spending a few days in each settlement preaching Islam as well as ministering to the sick. This could also help in attracting non-Muslims to Islam. Ordinary Muslims also should do this work, particularly among the low castes (Sikand, 1997).

So the influence of these great Deobandi thinkers and contemporaries on the method and ideology of the Tablighi work devised by Ilyas is clearly visible. However, while Ilyas was himself a devoted disciple of the leading Deobandi 'ulama and was committed to popularizing their teaching, he believed that the methods of communication that they had adopted- setting up *Deeni madaris* (religious schools), issuing fatwa or writing scholarly tomes-could hardly take them beyond a small, select circle. More or less, likewise Ahmad, Mumtaz (Ahmad, 1991), also wrote that Ilyas initially tried to establish a various network of masa'jid-based Islamic institutes to teach Muslims and Nau-Muslims about beliefs and practices of Islam but was soon disappointed that these schools were producing merely religious functionaries but not da'ies (preachers of Islam). So Ilyas devised a novel method of Tabligh favouring the method of direct oral communication (Sikand, 2002:72) appropriate and having many appeals to illiterate and ignorant Muslims like Mewati's (Lone, 2018b), whereby he changed the discourse of *tabligh* by making it an individual project, a shift from an 'ulama led project' where he viewed every Muslim as a missionary of Islam, as discussed above. Besides, while Ilyas himself subscribed to the Hanafi *mazahab* (school) as understood by the Deobandi's, he steered clear of intra- *mazahab* disputes among the

Sunnies, for the cultivation of faith, central to all four Sunni *mazahab*, was the main aim. He believed that the call of faith should be made to all Muslims, irrespective of the *mazhab*. Over time, the movement spawned by him was to make silence on inter- *mazahib* (plural of *mazhab*)differences a matter of policy, arguing that in matters of the detailed application of Islamic law, on which the *mazahib* differed from each other, Muslims could take recourse to the 'ulama of their own respective *mazhab* (Sikand, 2002: 69).

Two points, then, formed the core of Ilyas's Tablighi project, at least in its initial stages- strengthening faith and spreading awareness and practice of the basic Islamic ritual obligations (ibadat). Ilyas saw these as simply a means to the higher goal of bringing all affairs- ikhlaq (morals), mu'amulaat (transactions), ma'ashrat (society) and siyasat (the polity), that is, both the personal as well as public spheres, individual as well as social matters- in accordance with the dictates of the 'Shariah' (Haq, 1972:137). In several of his speeches and letters, Ilyas does appear to have referred to Islam in terms of a broader system extending beyond mere personal worship and ritual observance. Thus, in a letter to one Maulana Abdul Latif of Saharanpur, Ilyas wrote that the Meos of the Mewat must be told that it was essential to subordinate their panchayat's (community councils) and their trade to the dictates of the 'Shariah' and to take 'all decisions in that light', considering this to be the essence of Islam'. If they did not do this, he warned, their faith would remain most defective and could threaten to turn into pure infidelity (S. A. H. A. Nadwi, 1983). Though never explicitly repudiated, in actual practice, a distinct shift seems to have occurred away from the position in the years after Ilyas's death in 1944. It was largely the domain of the *'ibadat'* or personal piety that grew to become the immediate focus of Tablighi attention. For Ilyas and his activists, the primary aim was not so much detailed religious instruction as promoting a spiritual thirst among the Muslims to acquire knowledge of Islam so that, on that basis, they could begin to order their own lives in accordance with the injunctions of the 'Shariah'. The best way to do this, Ilyas suggested, was to step out of the un-Islamic environment of one's home and join a touring jama'at or fellow Muslims also on the same spiritual quest (Sikand, 2002:70).

At the very start of his campaign in the Mewat, Ilyas had not laid down any fixed or prescribed routine for the Tablighi activists. This was developed over time. In his own day, the activists were expected to spend at least three days every month away from their homes in a roving jamaat travelling to one or more Muslim locality or villages, spending their time there in teaching as well as learning. They were also encouraged to spend at least one chillah (a forty-day stretch of time) every year and at least three consecutive chillas's in a lifetime in jamaat's work. Later this came to be revised when Yousuf took as the amir (head) of the Tableeghi Jamaat after his father's death. Now the ideal Tablighi activist was one who spent eight months a year on jama'at, devoting only four months to family affairs and to earning a livelihood (Agwani, 1986: 47-48). Similarly, there are various accounts about the method of tabligh devised by Ilyas, one account suggests that it was divine inspiration and instruction. According to this account, after the failure of his *makatib* experience, Ilyas went to Madina, where he saw the Prophet Mohammad in a dream after few days of silent contemplation, asking Ilyas "move back to India and Allah will take work from you" (Sikand, 2002: 131), and thkarguzus 'Almighty Allah, taught Ilyas through a dream the method of the *'dawah'* (invitation) or the *'tariqi-i-tabligh'* [18] (Baliyavi, 2013: 52-53). Contrary to the above account, Ferozpuri mentions that Ilyas may have learned the method of *'tabligh'* from the 'Mewos' (Mewatis) themselves. Thus, he writes that one Hafeez Mohammad of Ferozpur-Namakk, son of Munshi Noor Baksh, a Meow disciple of Ilyas's elder brother Muhammad, had first formed a jamaat composed of seven men, besides him-who would sleep, cook and pray together and were inviting together the people around Feroozpur to offer prayers in the mosque (Ferozepuri, n.d., p.11). It is said that Ilyas was requested by the members of this group to visit their village- Ferozpur, to which Ilyas has been reported to have replied that their village- Feroozpur- Namak was an educated village where people very well take care of themselves. In turn, these groups of Meo-people have been reported to have replied, 'yes, of course, we are doing some work here. We invite people towards mosques through the 'ghast' and also admit our children in madrassa's (primary religious schools). Ilyas was very much inspired when he heard about the word 'ghast' and enquired about it. Ilyas was pleased to learn that few people were going house to house inviting people to mosque but had offered some suggestions to its improve it. Some of these were the appointment of 'head' or 'ameer' of the group to lead the group, appointment of a speaker or 'muttakalim' who's work would be to address the people, doing 'ghast' beyond Ferozpur in other villages also and not restricting the address to the prayers only but also talking, teaching and stressing about the importance of 'Tawheed' or 'kalima'[19] (Ferozepuri, n.d.-b: 16). This is how Ilyas has held view not only on the ideology of the method but also on the ideology of the content, and this is how the *tariqa tabligh* of the Tablighi Jamaat or faith movement of the Ilyas was developed.

Yet, according to another account, the method of the *tabligh* or '*tariq-i-tabligh*' was partly designed by Maulana Ilyas himself and was partially divinely inspired. Rahim Baksh, one of the intimate disciples of Maulana Mohamad Ilyas, mentions that Ilyas learned the method of the '*tabligh*' or 'da'wah' movement from Allah after his return from the second hajj when he entered into silent contemplation. In the dream, he was directed that he should make 'kalima' or 'article of faith' as the first principle of his 'da'wah' movement because the Prophet Muhamad's first lesson to his people was also the same, i.e. 'to attain blessings by the recitation of the 'kalima.' Then Maulana Ilyas made 'prayers' what he also called as 'sultan-i-ibadat' (emperor of worship) as the second principle of his 'da'wah' movement. Thereafter, Ilyas contemplated which aspect of Islam his own Deobandi elders and mentors had left untouched, which he could start with. In many parts of the United Provinces like Saharanpur and Deoband, religious knowledge was already being imparted by some notable Islamic personalities. For instance, Saed Ahmad was inviting people towards Islam through his lectures, Maulana Ashraf Ali Thanvi's religious instruction was already being done at Deoband and Saharanpur; Asraf Ali Thanvi had taken up writing Islamic books; Sa'ed Ahmad was propagating Islam through his lectures, and Hussain Ahmad Madani was serving Islam in the arena of politics. It was found by Ilyas that besides the 'article of faith'(kalima) and the 'prayers' the remaining four fundamentals of the 'six principles were not paid due attention by the scholars of his times, which they deserved. So he made his mind to stress on them also. Thus devising the method of the *'tabligh'* based on 'six principles,' he started his *'tablighi'* project among the Meows of Mewat. Here he was pressed by some Meo residents among his followers to write some instructional book about the basics or principles of *'tabligh'*. Initially, he was very unwilling to prescribe or recommend any such book because he was of the view that in the times of Prophets, there were no such books or printing presses, and the 'Sahaba' or the companions of Prophet Muhammad (PBUH) were engaged in 'da'wah' or *'tabligh'* orally 'by word of mouth'. However, upon the repeated requests made by his followers of Mewat, he instructed and advised some of his companions to pen down three texts and decided to commission them. These three books were: 'Fazaa'ill-i-Namaaz,' 'Faza'il-i-Tabligh' and 'Musalmanu ki Pastii ka Wahid Ilaaj' (The sole remedy for the plight of the Muslims).. The First two were compiled by Maulana Muhammad Zakariya (Ilyas's nephew and father-in-law of his son), and the third one was penned down by Ehtisham-ul Hassan Kandhalwi (cousin and brother in Law of Ilyas) [20]. This is how the unique *tariqa-i-tabligh* of the Tableeghi Jamaat or the 'Faith Renewal Movement' of the Maulana Ilyas came to be developed.

However, after Ilyas's death, the influence of Muhammad Zakariya as the chief ideologies of the movement grew considerably. He and Maulana Yousuf, Ilyas's son and successor as leader of the Tablighi Jamaat seem to have enjoyed a particularly close relationship. Consequently, over time, the Tableeghi Jamaat came to developed an elaborate set of texts of faz'il compiled by Maulana Zakariya (Zakkriyya, 2015). This was published in two volumes, the Faza'il-i-'Amal (The Blessings of Pious Acts' also known as the Tablighi Nisaab or the 'Tablighi Syllabus'). The first volume of this text is divided into six sections- the Hikayat-i-Sahabah or the stories about the companion's of the Prophet, written at the request of the Zakariya's spiritual mentor, Abdul Qadir Raipuri; and other five sections dealing with the rewards of reciting the Quran, offering prayers, remembering God, participating in *tabligh,* and observing the Ramadhan fasts, respectively. The second volume contains various stories relating to the rewards of charity. Several of these chapters on the *faza'il* had been prepared under Ilyas's instructions. Later the Faza'il-i-Amal was supplemented with another set of texts, the Hayat-us Sahaba ('Lives of the Companions') compiled by Maulana Yousuf. (Kandhalawi, 1981). This book consists of several short stories based on the lives of the Prophet, his companions and other pious Muslims. Like the Faza'il-i-Amal it was read out in Tablighi circles and gatherings and was to serve as a guide for instruction. Tablighi activists were discouraged by Tableeghi Jamaat leaders from reading any literature besides these two set of texts, other works of Zakriyya, and the writings of another Tablighi ideologue, Manzur Numani of Lucknow (Ahmad, M 1991:516).

Narrating stories from these books, particularly the Faza'il-i-'Amal, emerged in the years after Ilyas's death as a central ritual act in the Tablighi tal'lim (education) sessions for the *muballigheen.* One person would read aloud a story from the books of faza'il, while the others sitting on the floor in a semi-circle around him would listen attentively. The purpose of the narration of the faz'il, besides its use as a pedagogical device, was to serve as a major incentive for the listeners to strengthen their own faith, to emulate in their 'own personal lives, particularly in the realm of ritual practice, the examples of the early pious Muslims, and above all, to actively participate in the work of the *tabligh* in the hope of the divine reward (S. A. H. A. Nadwi, 1983: 101). Great blessings were said to follow from performing even the seemingly simplest of ritual acts. Thus, for instance, it was said that if one were merely to recite the first part of the kalima, 'there is no God but Allah', a hundred times a day, one would earn the reward of 'releasing ten slaves from among the children of the prophet Ismail' (Bulandsahri, 1989: 15). Likewise, if a person who, while 'on the path of Allah' (i.e., while on *tabligh*), were to recite a thousand verses of the Quran, God would include him among the prophets (anbiya), the truthful ones (*saaddiqeen*), the martyrs (the *shuhada*) and the pure (*salehin*) (Ferozepuri, n.d.-b., p. 13). By simply using a stick toothbrush (*miswak*) one was promised that the value of his prayer would be multiplied to between 99 and 400 times because it was the sunnah of the Prophet to do so, and for bringing back to life and practice of the Muhammad, no matter how small, that had fallen into disuse, Allah would provide immensely heavenly reward (Hussain, n.d., p.18). Regularly participating in *tabligh* tours itself would, it was claimed, will bring great reward in Allah's account books. Thus for each good deed that a person did 'while out struggling in the path of the Allah', he would be bestowed with the reward for 7 000,000 such deeds according to Mahmud ul-Hasan, chief Mufti, Dru-ul Ulum Deoband (Vellore, n.d., p. 18). For each word uttered while 'inviting others to the truth during the *tabligh* "da'wah' ' journey, one would receive blessings equal to that for an entire year's worship (Haqqani, n.d., p. 10). According to another report, the reward for this was the blessings that accrue for 49 crore of such deeds (M. R. S. Qasmi, 1996). If one were to die while on tabligh one would earn a place in the heaven just one step below to that of the prophets (Bulandsahri, 1989: 25).

Although the first edition of the complete Faza'il-i-Amal did not appear until after Ilya's death, sections of it were already in use in Tablighi circles by the 1940s with Ilyas's approval. Nadwi writes that it was a sign of Ilyas's 'intelligence' that he understood clearly that the world 'runs on the power of the profit motive'. With the search for the gain being the driving force behind every human action, Ilyas, he says, believed that Muslims could be encouraged to actively participate in the work of the *tablighi* if they were told of the grand promises of eternal joy in heaven that they would have if they walked on the path of the God. Hence he writes, Ilyas commissioned Zakkariyya to write the books of the Faza'il for the instruction of the Tablighi activists (S. A. H. A. Nadwi, 1983). Narrating the divine reward for the pious acts, believed Ilyas, was more immediate necessity than imparting the detailed instruction in the masa'il- detailed matters related to the Islamic law because it was through the faza'il that 'belief in the recompense of actions was made firm' men were attracted to do good deeds and, consequently, 'motivated to find out the masa'il themselves (ibid: 252). Thus narrating the faza'il (blessings or rewards of pious acts/ deeds) such as reciting of Kalima or Quran and acting upon them, from the Tablighi literature for the renewal of faith among the Muslims also forms one of the important ideological characteristics of the Tableeghi Jamaat. Besides this, in the above pages, the important points which have been highlighted characterizing the ideology of the Tableeghi Jamaat are:

- **(a)First**, the focus of the Tablighi 'da'wah' project is only on the Muslims (or neo-Muslims) and not on non-Muslims. It's based on the principle that it's better to save and secure Muslims first who are in danger before inviting non-Muslims to Islam. It's based yet on another principle, as advocated by Tableeghi Jamaat, that Muslims should first practice Islam themselves well before going out to preach to others or non-Muslims. And, that is also why that Ilyas preferred it to call *'tahreek Imaan'* [21] or faith renewal (or purification) movement.
- **(b) Second**, the ideological characteristic is that Ilyas held the view 'that every Muslim is a missionary', including women. In other words, he viewed 'da'wah' obligatory on every Muslim and not just only on *'Ulama's* and Sofi's. Besides, unlike Islamists like Jamaat Islami, who mostly focus, on educated, literate, and middle-class sections of Islamic society, Tableeghi Jamaat 'da'wah' project has followers and members from all sections

of the society, including illiterate and even handicapped like deaf people, taking part actively in the activities of the Tablighi movement. Likewise, Mumtaz Ahmad (Ahmad, M 1991) writes, 'Tableeghi Jamaat has followers from all sections of the Muslim society. It is, thus, like a gross-root movement. In contrast to this, Jamaat Islami, support base mostly consists of educated people and lower-middle-class sections of Muslims'.

- **(c)Third**, unless *'Ulama'* (the learned) and Sufi's participate in Tablighi tours and teach people Islam practically on the principle of learning by doing, their mere speeches will not benefit people much.

- **(d)Fourth**, the gap between the 'ulama and ordinary Muslims is the main reason for the irreligiosity and apostasy of the Muslims.

- **(e)Fifth**, ghast or travelling from community to community, or home to home while inviting people to the mosque is the best way for the renewal of faith or keeping Islam live. Or in other words, joining the Tablighi tours is the best way to learn, practice, and preach Islam.

- **(f)Sixth**, the Tablighi activists must conform to the *'Shariah,'* Quran and Sunnah while preaching or carrying out daily activities, at least according to the ideology of Ilyas, the founder of the Jamaat.

Besides, in continuation to the above, the other important points which characterize the ideology of the Tablighi Jamaat, which need elaboration, are:

- **(g)Seventh**, an important ideological characteristic of Tableeghi Jamaat is their differentiation between religious affairs from worldly. In other words, Tableeghi Jamaat makes a separation between this-worldly (*dunyavi*) and otherworldly (*deenvi*) matters. Islamic groups like Jamaat-i Islami, which see Islam as an all-embracing worldview or ideology, recognize no distinction between the spiritual and temporal realms. For them, Islam is all-encompassing, including both personal devotions, individual behaviour, and worship, as well as the ordering and regulation of social affairs. For them, the *'Duniya'*, this world, cannot be separated from the deen. In fact, this *Duniya* is the arena where din must be made manifest and actualized. On the other hand, the Tablighi position on what constitutes the deen is ambiguous, to say the least. There is some evidence, as we have seen above, that Ilyas himself did see the din in more holistic and inclusive terms in a manner not dissimilar to contemporary Islamists. However, after Ilyas's death, there seems to have been a gradual shift in this perception regarding this, at least in actual practice. This may have been due to the changed political context of post -1947 India when Muslims found themselves a hopelessly outnumbered and increasingly threatened minority for whom the grand goal of establishing an Islamic state obviously appeared almost impossibility. Consequently, the Tablighi focus as it came to be developed after Ilyas's death fitted in with the demands and constraints of the new political order. There was focus on the realm of personal worship, interpersonal behaviour, and the sphere of Muslim personal law as recognized by the Indian constitution, and increasingly projecting in actual practice, if not in theory, these alone as the domain of the deen. Today when pressed by their detractors, Tablighi leaders will often reply that they recognize no distinction between the *'Deen'* and the *'Duniya'* and they, too, are, in their own way, are working to bring the whole way of man's life-spiritual as well as this-worldly, private as well as public- in accordance with the laws of the *'Deen'* (Sikand, 2002: 84-85). In actual practice, however, many Tablighi activists do tend to make a distinction between the din, as rituals, moral behaviour, and personal worship, on the one hand, and the *'Duniya'*, on the other. Yoginder Sikand has quoted 'that a government intelligence officer stresses, the activists of the movement, 'either talk about the things in the sky (heaven) or the world beneath the earth (hell). They do not talk about things on the surface of the earth (ibid: 85).

The deen, then, is, in practice, usually seen not simply apart from the 'Duniya' or world. Rather, it is often, at least in common Tablighi perception, set up against the *'Duniya'* itself. Consequently, worldly engagement comes to be seen with considerable distaste, and so Tablighi activists must constantly be aware that, as the Prophet himself has declared that 'this world and whatever is in it is cursed by Allah with the exception of prayers and dhikr (remembrance of God) and the religious scholar and the religious student (Bulandsahri, 1989: 7). Ilyas had himself often prayed to God, 'oh God! Keep me alive in the state of indigence and grant me death in the state of indigence and raise me up on the day of resurrection in the company of the indigent (S. A. H. A. Nadwi, 1983:167).

As a result of this distinction is made between the *Deen* and the *'Duniya'*, the din comes to be seen by many Tablighi activists as more or less synonymous with obligatory ritual practices and personal conduct, although this may not have been what Ilyas himself believed. The *'dunyavi'* is then all that what lies outside of what, for many Muslims, is this narrow understanding of the *Deen*. Tablighi activists believe while in this world people do have to engage in *'Dunyavi'* affairs simply to survive, such involvement should, as for as possible, be limited to the very basic minimum, for the world and all that is in it is but a snare, a 'toilet or a 'prison-cell (Alam, op. cit.: 648). Thus, Muslims are exhorted to follow the path of the companions of Muhammad, many of whom, a leading Tablighi ideologue approvingly says, had so much little concern for this world that they 'could not even distinguish between a salt and a camphor or between a chapati and a handkerchief or between an apricot seed and a stone' (Baliyavi, n.d.: 60-61). Tablighi activists must constantly engage in the inner struggle against the ego to suppress all worldly desires,, including the thirst for worldly power (M. K. Nizami, n.d., M. K. Nizami, 1993: 10). Like the prophet, they must keep their houses empty of all worldly goods and build up spiritual treasures for themselves in heaven instead. The pleasures of the world are illusory, for life on earth is just a fleeting movement when set against the eternity of the hereafter. Hence, instead of making success in this evanescent world the object of one's labours, one should devote oneself entirely to accumulating enough divine reward to earn the eternal pleasures of heaven (Sikand, 2002:86).

- **(h)Eighth**, closely related to the *'Deen-Duniya'* division, Tabighi ideology also makes a distinction between the 'ibadat and the rest of the deen, as understood in its broader sense. While this does not seem to have been the case with Ilyas himself, Tableeghi Jamaat activists today generally claim as their focus of immediate attention only the former, along with the realm of personal behaviour. Islamists generally see 'ibadat as the observance of the shari'ah in every aspect of personal as well as collective life, from prayers and fasting to the conduct of state affairs and international relations. In contrast, the general Tablighi understanding of the term is limited only to the sphere of personal devotion and ritual obligations. It is only after Muslims perfect their *ibadat* (worship), as here understood, and bring Islamic morality into their 'personal' dealings with others that it's believed they can run their attention to building society as a whole following the teachings of Islam. Political power, if at all God-Allah decides to pass it on to the Muslims, can only be had as a final culmination in this long-drawn process, but in no way should Muslims actively seek to acquire it (Ferozepuri, n.d.-a.:24).

That stage may be long in coming, though. Indeed, in practice, it is often indefinitely postponed, with Muslims constantly falling prey to all sorts of worldly temptations. Hence, the need to repeatedly stress the importance of the faith and personal devotion, to the exclusion of much else, over and over again lest the foundations of the faith begin to weaken. This is why the same message-of cultivating the faith, conquer one's basic self, regularly saying one's prayers, abiding faithfully by the six principles, and so on- is constantly sought to be reinforced through lectures and in tracts penned by Tablighi leaders, as a consequence of which they all have a uniform and almost an unvarying content (Sikand, 2002: 87).

- **(i)Ninth,** unlike many Islamists though not all, Tableeghi Jamaat ideology, oppose *Ijtihad* [22] (ibid: 4), show a strong aversion to the use of science and reason (Agwani, 1986: 48) in interpreting religious matters, and call for strict *taq'lid* or strict adherence to Islamic jurisprudence as developed over the centuries by the 'Scholars or *'Ulama'*of the schools of Sunni Islamic law. Although the Tableeghi Jamaat has its roots in the South Asian Deobandi movement owing allegiance to Hanafi School, it permits non-Hanafi followers, all of whom are Sunni, to follow their own respective schools of jurisprudence (Metcalf, 1982). Islamists are often critical of the traditional 'ulama for being hopelessly out of touch with modern realities, for their outdated, obsessive concern with rituals, and for their alleged complicity with 'un-Islamic' rulers' The Tableeghi Jamaat enjoins upon its followers to follow strictly in the path of the 'ulama of the established schools of law, recognizing no possibility of reinterpreting *fiq'h*to suit the needs of changing contexts (Shakir, 1972: 51). The Tableeghi Jamaat, unlike many Islamist groups, envisages no room for ijtihad or the use of independent reasoning in adapting Muslim law to modern concerns and problems. While Islamists generally enthusiastically embrace modern science, Tableeghi Jamaat does not (Sikand, 2002: 3). Thus, for instance, an important ideologue of the Tableeghi Jamaat, namely Muhammad Zakariya Kandhalwi (1898-1982), is reported have described the 'perfect scholar' as one who has learnt those subjects that are used for the 'next world' and shuns those that are not. 'in our ignorance, he wrote, ' we regard all such knowledge as a success which results in worldly gains, but in fact, all such knowledge is merely ignorance' (Agwani, 1986: 48). A strong strand of Tablighi opinion still continues in this tradition, and the Tableeghi Jamaat is, in fact, explicitly hostile to the use of reason and science in religious matters. It is also vehemently opposed to modern Muslim attempts to fashion a creative theology and reinterpret Islamic jurisprudence to address issues of contemporary concern, such as, for instance, women's rights write's Sikand (Sikand, 2002:4)

- **(j) Tenth**, one of the most important ideological characteristics or belief of the Tablighi Jamaat is that, if Islam has to progress, rather Ilyas's faith renewal movement in its 'da'wah' activity, then it must be divorced from involving in the politics or any political affair. Thus they advocate the separation of religion-Islam from politics. For instance, Anwarul Haq (Haq, 1972:72) writes, 'that Shah Wali-u'llah regarded political authority as indispensable for the community, whereas Ilyas, strictly kept his movement for getting into politics'. While as some Sufi orders in the past have called for diversion from politics, and few religious leaders did practice the same whenever there happened to be a government in power which they did not approve of. However, Ilyas, perhaps for the first time in the history of Muslim religious movements of India, made it a fundamental principle of his 'da'wah' work. Otherwise, generally in other Muslim countries and particularly in India, religious and social reform movements ultimately tend to become involved in politics while political movements appealed to the masses only when they took a religious grab. (ibid, 167).

Tablighi Jamaat ideologists are of the view that it is illogical, irrational, rather a wastage of time when Muslims desire, try or struggle to establish Shari'ah state or Islamic state, in the circumstance when they 'themselves do nothing to follow shari'ah in their personal lives. This view of them contrasts the ideology of many Islamists like Jamaat-i-Islami. Unlike Tableeghi Jamaat, they are of the view that if Muslims wish to enforce 'Shariah' in their personal or collective affairs of all the Muslims, then they must struggle or strive for the Islamic state. In other words, they are of the view that the Islamic State is a necessary condition to observe or enforce 'Shariah' both collective affairs of Muslims as well as in personal affairs. As Yoginder Sikand (Sikand, 2002: 2), while quoting Umer Palanpuri (a Tablighi leader), mentions, 'that it is silly to desire for an Islamic state or to capture political power when Muslims don't conform to 'Shariah' in their personal lives. Thus, the 'bottom-up approach of the Tablighi Jamaat where they focus on self-reform first, is quite contrasted to the 'top-down approach of Islamist groups who regard 'Islamic state' as an indispensable condition, rather a precondition for the enforcement of shari'ah in the individual and collective affairs of the Muslims. Sikand, in this regard, has talked an interesting thing, he says, while the plan or ideology of establishing 'Shariah' or Islamic state by the Islamist groups is based on the 'political community' which was founded by Prophet Muhammad in the 6th century in Madina, that of the Tableeghi Jamaat's ideology is based on the early years of Prophets life in Makkah (or Mecca), where he placed focus on 'inviting people to Islam' (Lone, 2018b).

However, it has been said that Ilyas's aversion to politics arose from his bitter experience in Saudi Arabia in 1938 when Saudi authorities peremptorily turned down his request for permission to do preaching work at Mecca and Madina. Thus realizing out of shock, that while he was able to freely undertake 'da'wah' or preaching in British-India ruled by key enemies of Islam, but was denied the same in the centre of Islam (Agwani, 1986: 50-51), he might have felt that if Islam has to make any sort of progress, amid the circumstances when aims of Islam and modern political authority are quite contrasting, it needed to be separated from politics (Haq, 1972: 170). His political ideas were almost similar to those of Syed Ahmad Khan, who had also objected to the involvement of Muslims in the Indian National Congress or freedom struggle because of the fact that the Muslim community had much suffered from that and many unfair charges were labelled against them. He did not wish to get the same repeated. His purpose of advising Muslims to keep away from politics was to safeguard them. Ilyas also adopted the same policy amid the conflicting socio-political atmosphere. And because of this apolitical nature, Muslims of diverse political affiliations or views were able to join and work together in his movement. Thus he strictly avoided political discussions or involvement and instructed his followers and workers to do the same. He firmly believed that political power or government could never be the goal of Muslims. If they achieved political authority while walking on the path of the Prophet, they need not avoid that responsibility, but this should never be their objective. And when the movement acquired momentum, Ilyas forbade political discussions among the preaching groups. As individuals, the workers were free to hold their own political views and to participate in political affairs, provided they did not import them into their religious endeavours or make use of their preaching activity for political ends (ibid.:170-71).

However, Mumtaz Ahmad notes that while Ilyas stayed aloof from politics so as to devote his entire attention to 'tabligh'. He was not opposed to the work of Muslim groups participating in the political arena and, indeed, saw their work as complementing his. He writes that the Tableeghi Jamaat seems to have adopted a policy of strict political aloofness only after the partition of India in 1947. This he attributes to the changed political situation in India after 1947 when the government and Hindu majority viewed any attempt at the political assertion of Muslims, qua Muslims, as a threat to national security. Another factor he cites is the expansion in this period of the Tableeghi Jamaat to new pastures in South-East Asia and Europe, where any political assertion on the part of Muslims would have been looked at with grave suspicion (Ahmad, 1991). In the days of Ilyas, he strongly advocated separate identity for Muslims not just only in dress or attitude but also in political participation, particularly amid the circumstances when they are subjected to grave social and political marginalization. For instance, Yoginder, Sikand writes,'the role of dress and external appearance as community boundary markers, separating meows from Hindus, enabling in the process of constructing distinct Meo- Muslim identity. Such a separate identity assumes particular salience at crucial times, such as elections to local body councils, the state legislatures, and the national parliament when Islam is often invoked by Meo politicians to garner Meo support, especially in the cases where the opposing candidates are non-Meows. The Tablighi Jamaat has an interesting dual purpose of playing in Mewati Politics. On the one hand, because it remains aloof from party politics, it allows space for the Meows to associate with secular political forces, this being no small advantage in a context wherein, as a result of the Muslims being a marginalized minority, Islamic or Muslim communal political parties do not appear as a viable option. On the other hand, Tableeghi Jamaat provides key Islamic symbols around which Meo politicians seek to garner Meo votes in a political system where communities generally tend to vote together en bloc. In this regard, it is interesting to note that the vast gatherings that the Tableeghi Jamaat holds periodically in Mewat, which attracts thousands of Meos, provides the Meows with an arena for the display of strength, a symbol of assertion of considerable political in the context wherein the Meos find themselves a beleaguered minority. More generally, the links which the Tableeghi Jamaat opens up for the Meows with the wider Muslim world and, indeed, with the Muslim ummah as a whole, provides, in symbolic terms, a crucial sense of empowerment in a situation of considerable social and political marginalization (Sikand, 2002: 167-68).

This view that Ilyas saw Islam as a broader system- an all-embracing ideology including subordinating politics to "Shariah" is proved by his letter, in which he wrote and instructed his activists that Islam is a broader system, beyond mere individual worship and ritual observance, thus they must subordinate their trade, panchayats and all decisions' to the dictates of 'Shariah' or Islam. Otherwise, the objection, of which he warned them, may turn them into pure infidelity (S. A. H. A. Nadwi, 1983, p. 115). Troll (1994, p.129) says 'that Ilyas was of the view that if an individual was conforming strictly to the holy law and rituals of Islam was ultimately leading to the foundation of Islamic political structures

(Troll. Christian W, 2019). Similarly, Khalid Masud (2000: 99) maintains that it is wrong to say that Ilyas had no regard for politics or having political plans. The political aims were included in the project, but they were not the goal to be sought for; instead, they were kept as an addition, which would come by default as an addition(Masud, 2000). However, Sikand notes that Tableeghi Jamaat's position changed after the death of the Ilyas in 1944, whereby it focused on all matters to the dictates of sharia, tilted towards individual piety and ibadat (Sikand, 2002: 70).

- **(k) Eleventh**, the Tableeghi Jamaat dislike writing about them and shun publicity. There is an 'extreme paucity of literature or written material that can be said to represent the official position of Tableeghi Jamaat' (ibid: 4). They say that even the prophet and his beloved companions invited people towards Islam directly by word of mouth. Thus Tablighi activists must follow them as their model while in '*tabligh*', and should avoid western models of communication for that they badly affect spiritualism and divert one's attention from basics to unnecessary and irrelevant things. Besides, they see Islam as not something to be read, talked or written about, but above all, '*amaali kaam*,' that is, practical work- sought, struggled, followed, and practised practically, not just paying lip service. They also believe that personal communication is far more effective means of putting the 'Tablighi message across than the written word, for it allows face–t-o face interaction between the missionary and the person he is addressing, making it possible for the former to modify his approach to suit the temperament of each listener. Besides, Tablighi's aversion to literature ties in with the low profile that it intentionally seeks for itself, seeing publicity as something hostile and irritating. As Yoginder Sikand, quoting the British Tablighi respondent saying, 'our motto is no talk, no literature and no expenditure (na charcha,na parcha, na kharcha)' (Sikand, 2002: 5-6).

Similarly, Maulana Wahiddudin Khan (Khan, 1986:40), writes, 'the Maulana Ilyas disapproved the prevalent system of publicity. He wrote in one of his letters that, 'to make his mission public, the advertising media, newspapers, advertisements, posters and so on should be avoided as far as possible, for the whole of our work is unconventional. The real way of working is to address people individually, to impart education by approaching people, and to form groups of people to work together. His disliking for the publicity was so extreme that none of the copies of his letters was available after his death, though he frequently wrote letters. However, the same writer mentions that Ilyas hostility towards the literature or publicity changed after the success of the movement, which he felt was initially the need of the hour. Under the heading 'the Use of the Pen' the author, quoting Ilyas writing in one of his letters, thus mentions (ibid.,: 30), 'so far I have not approved of the use of the pen in this work, but now the time has come to use this medium. Not only have I not approved of it, but I have also prohibited people from using it. But now I want them to write as much as they can. You must consult other senior members in this regard. They were consulted, but they did not agree with his opinion. On hearing of their disagreement, the Maulana again observed: 'Actually, in the beginning, we were in danger of being seriously misunderstood. People were not prepared even to listen to us. It was in those circumstances imperative for us to approach them personally and, by our example, impress upon them our objectives. If we had taken recourse to write, people would have misinterpreted the mission. And then, when its application went awry, they would have rejected it altogether as worthless. That is why they deliberately avoided the help of the news media. But now, owing to our devoted volunteers who have worked hard to spread the mission among the people, it has become as clear as day. The people now are themselves flocking to us to learn more and more. We have a large number of devoted people who can be sent to any part of the country where the need arises. There is no point in our sticking to the initial method of working when the times have changed. I recommend, therefore, that you take up your pens to further the cause of the mission' (W. Khan, 1986: 30). Thus it can be said that earlier Ilyas showed hostility to media, or written material about the aims, ideology or concern of the mission, only to avoid its wrong impression and misinterpretation by the masses. So, in the beginning, it was wise and need of the hour to approach people directly, to be aware and inform them properly about the Tablighi mission. Now when the message has reached a large number of people and when now large numbers of people are flocking towards the movement, there is nothing wrong in abandoning the initial method 'showing aversion' to pen, media or publicity. Thus Ilyas, in the later stage of his life, when the *'tabligh* mission' reached quite a success, approved writing or publicity about his mission or the movement he launched for Islamic revival among Muslims.

In this backdrop, that is why, Sikand notes that in recent years several slim tracts and books, mainly in Urdu but increasingly in other languages, have been published, which present Tablighji doctrines in a concise form. However, the same author notes that these publications don't represent the official position of the 'jamaat' because they have not been officially issued by the Tableeghi Jamaat. Written in simple language and generally low priced makes them affordable to a large proportion of 'Tableeghi Jamaat' activists who come from lower middle class or poor backgrounds. These books are mainly concerned with the principles, aims and methods of the Tableeghi Jamaat; and show little interest in exploring the history of the movement, to which 'Tableeghi Jamaat ideologists' show strong aversion. They believe history is mostly written about the fame and worldly glory, to which every believer must hate and fight. They see the world or 'worldly desires' like a 'toilet' or a 'prison cell' and maintain that a true believer must constantly engage in battle with worldly desires or fame, and every individual desire should be for winning the pleasure of God Allah, not for any worldly attainment. Consequently thus, Tablighi Jamaat leaders dislike others for writing about them (Sikand, 2002: 6-8). Likewise, Tariq Abdullah (Tariq, 1995:22), while quoting Enamul Hassan, the third 'ameer' of the 'Tableeghi Jamaat' arguing, that, the *'Ulama'* have always sought to conceal and save themselves from glory and fame'. Because of this, he says, they would write books 'only under the direst circumstances' or when approached by a disciple to pen a treatise on 'an important point of religious law'.

Thus it can be concluded from the above that Tablighi Jamaat shows hatred to publicity to avoid worldly fame as it affects the basics of the movement and spirituality of the members. However, the books are allowed to write about the main concern, principles, aims and methods of the movement. Moreover, Ilyas himself favoured direct, oral and personal communication modelled on the methodology of Prophet and his companions; and, also communication between the members within the movement is largely oral [23]

- **(1) Twelfth**, about the impact of 'Sufism' or its involvement on the ideology of the Tableeghi Jamaat, Anwarul Haq (Haq, 1972), has given a detailed and fine analysis of Sufism on the work, methodology and ideology of Ilyas, which (Sufism) he says Ilyas has adopted with certain changes. He comes to the conclusion that Ilyas has adopted and advocated only such Sufi practices like zikr, *chillah,*(forty days) and *muraqabah,* which conform to *'Shariah'*, and like Sheikh Ahmad Sirhindi and other orthodox Sufis, has rejected any Sufi practice or any mystic experience like sima [24], amulets and zikr-i-jali [25] which do not conform to the dictates of the Quran and the Sunnah. Khalid Masud (2000, xl), is of view that Tablighi Jamaat is more like a reformist movement of ulama's and does not look like a Sufi movement. Sanyal (1996: 97-127), maintains, there is nothing like Sufism found in the Tablighi Jamaat, the leadership of which belong to the 'Sabriya' branch of the Chasttiya order – which is 'non-mystical. Instead, he says, the element of Sufism is found among the Tableeghi Jamaat's rival school, that is, among the

'Barelvi's' which have an affiliation to some other branches' of the Chastiyaa order, like 'qadriya' or 'naqshbandiya'. Similarly, Kepel (2000:42) has viewed the 'Tableeghi Jamaat' as hostile to Sufism because of its strict objection to the 'cult' or sect of tombs. However, according to certain scholars that some elements of Sufism were introduced in the movement to make it successful on the one hand and to avoid its bad impression among the people on the other. Besides, Ilyas adopted Sufi terms and practices such as *zikr, muraqabah, kankhah* and *chillah*, with certain changes, to popularize Sufism and create a better understanding of it among the masses

Besides, the Sufi terms and practices with some changes, used by Maulana Mohammad Ilyas for better understanding of Sufism and to popularize it or its true version were *zikr, kankhah, muraqaba and chillah*; and at the same time he sought to eliminate the abuses which had crept in Sufism.(Haq, 1972: 72-73). Similarly, Troll (1985) and Gaborieau (1986), are of the view that the success of the movement is mainly linked to the 'Sufi charisma' called *'nisbat'*, which has *'intiqaled'* or transferred, passed or shifted from Ilyas to Yusuf. Thus to them, the success of the movement is based on the transference of Sufi charisma (intiqal-i-nisbat) from the predecessor to successor. However, Gaborieau maintains that the 'tag' of Sufism is used by Tableeghi Jamaat, on the one hand; for a good impression and to get legitimacy, and on the other hand; for not to be labelled as fundamental movement or a movement leading or arousing sectarian clashes (Lone, 2018b), and

- **(m) Lastly, Thirteenth,** and more importantly, in its course of *'da'wah'* work, Ilyas required Tablighi activists to strictly follow 'six principles' or which in Tablighi circles are commonly referred to as *'chai baatie'*. These six principles represent a sort of 'ideological structure' of the Tablighi Jamaat, which is fundamental for the renewal of faith among the Muslims at the basic level, which will help in their knowledge, cultivation of faith, moral and spiritual development. (Lone, 2018; Sikand, 1986; Mumtaz, 1991). However, some scholars like Agwani (1986: 43-45), Haq (1973:142) and Lone (2018), that Ilyas required seven essentials for the Tablighi activists to concentrate on while in a *'da'wah'* or preaching tour. These six principles *'chai baatie'* viz. i. *shahadah,* ii. *namaz,* iii. *Ilm-o zikr,* iv. *Ikram-i-Muslim,* v. *ikhlas-i-niyat* and vi. *Tafrigh waqt* is the fundamental one, and the 'seventh' one, that is, *tarq-i-layani* is of a general character. In all, these could be referred to as 'seven essentials' containing six fundamentals. (ibid, 2018). However, Haq (Haq, 1972:142-45) has referred to these principles or essentials as 'six positive' and one negative, while as Maulana Wahiduddin Khan (W. Khan, 1986: 24) maintained, that Maulana Ilyas's plan was comprised of 'six important aims'. Mumtaz Ahmad (Ahmad, 1991) is of the view that Maulana Ilyas's plan comprised of small, mobile units of Tablighi Jamaat activists, containing around and at least 10 to 12 members, who were required to travel to various villages for preaching. Here they were to present their *'da'wah'* messages according to the six demands.

These principles, which lie at the base of Tablighi 'da'wah' ideology, have been discussed systematically in the following pages.

- (1). **Article of Faith or Kalima or Shadah or testimony**: The first one is the 'kalima' which is as follows: *'La Illha Illa'Llahu, Muhamamadu-r-Rasool-ull Llah'* meaning 'that there is no God but Almighty Allah, and 'Muhammad'(PBUH) is the last messenger and slave of Allah'. Ilyas's message gives prime importance to the Kalima; to believe in the reality that there is no deity but God Almighty Allah, that he alone is the Creator and the Nourisher of the universe, and the truth had been made manifest through His messenger, the Prophet Muhammad. When one recites these words: that there is no 'deity' but God 'Allah' and the Prophet Muhammad (PBUH) is the messenger and slave of Allah, it amounts to expressing one's inner feelings of conviction of the truth, of these words. It also proclaims one's determination to follow a path based on the firm conviction that God Allah is the only real existence, the centre of all our complete trust. This proclamation is an expression of an all-pervasive feeling within one of having at last found the true way of life and also the source from which truth emanates- the only source whose guidance is worthy of trust.

Trust and conviction are, in fact, the source of all revolution, be it religious or secular. A history of revolution tells us that it was the courage of conviction-right or wrong-in certain souls, which has made history. For instance, Maulana Wahidudin Khan (W. Khan, 1986: 25), gives the example of communism, though was based on partial truth, yet some political, economic or nationalistic truths or convictions aroused and inspired people to such a degree that they concentrated all their potentialities and energies on making it known to people. One can then imagine what the strength of such a conviction would be like when based on truth in the real sense of the word. When such truths are firmly implanted in one's heart and mind, like a divine fervour, one can guess what enormous benefits can result. The true faith, over which the people have put their total trust in God Allah, has the potential to move all mankind. The *Kalimah* is thus the essence of religion- the greatest power on the earth. The movement can be thus appropriately called a *'kalimah movement'* (ibid., 26).

The Kalima has to be memorized correctly, paying particular attention to pronunciation at least uttered correctly. The emphasis is on understanding its significance as a divine command. The article has broadly two aspects: one having the belief that God Almighty Allah is an alone deity worthy of worship; and second, having a belief that the last Messenger of Allah's way, that is, the Prophet's Mohammad's way, is the right way and final way to worship or establish a connection with God. In other words 'kalima' has two parts that are, belief and testimony in one Allah and; testimony and obedience to the Prophet. Besides the 'kalima' is sometimes also referred to as 'faith' or 'emaan'. The word 'emaan' in Arabic describing faith literally means 'believing in the words of the messenger with full conviction and certainty. The word of faith 'kalima' thus means expressing belief in the message of Allah, conveyed through His Messenger with full conviction, confidence and certainty (Haq, 1972; Kandhalavi, 2009).

- (2). **Prayers.** The second important part of the Maulans Ilyas's call is to prayer or namaz or salaa't. Here Tableeghi Jamaat activists learn about the various details and rules of namaz, the obligatory and other prayers, as well as rules about the ritual purity. Just as 'kalima' enjoys the main position in one's thoughts and feelings, so does prayer in ones practical life. The real significance of prayer lies in men diverting all his attention to God and making contact with him through sense perceptions. Through them the worshipper bows before his Lord, placing his forehead on the Ground, he testifies to his own lowliness as opposed to Gods exalted nature. He presents himself as Gods servant. He stands before God, bows down to him, and prostrates himself before Him, in a practical demonstration of submission to God. It is when one humbles oneself before the Lord that one is in a position to meet Him; for one discovers God on a level of humility, not on a level of pride or egotism. One's soul then undergoes such an experience that one can feel the blessing of God descending upon one. Such an experience, which defies description, gives a new dimension to human personality. The worshiper consciously realizes how helpless and powerless he is before God. Humility and modesty alone befit a servant of God. In the process, arrogance and haughtiness, which are the source of most evils, vanish into thin air.

Prayer, as mentioned in the Quran, keeps one away from evils and shameful practices and is the only manifest difference between a Muslim and a kafir [26]. With every prayer, man expresses his servitude before God and promises to Him that he will try to lead his life as His devoted servant. It reminds him of the day of reckoning. If a man is true to his words, his life can be transformed by them.

Besides, in the first principle, the pledge of worship and obedience to Allah and His Prophet are fulfilled through prayers and prayers are the first practical step towards proof of one's faith. Prayer also has two parts, external and internal. The former consists in performing the preludes to prayer such as ablutions, involving all the acts which the Prophet and his Companions performed. These are to be done exactly the same way as Prophet did them. In the internal sense, prayer is to strive for perfect submissiveness in every single act which will create in the individual the quality of abstention from vile deeds. This is the real meaning of prayers (Kandhalavi, 2009).

- (3). **Knowledge and remembrance of God- Almighty Allah (called Dhikr).** The third essential principle is acquiring knowledge and remembering God all the time. In Tablighi parlance, this principle is referred to as 'ilm-o-zikr'. Every day a part of the morning and evening hours is to be spent for this purpose. There are general and special forms of remembrance. As regards the former, a Muslim is expected to recite the tasbiha [27] (one hundred times) of the third 'kalimah' and two tasbih each of the durood [28] and istighafar[29]. A specific time is to be fixed for these devotions. Besides, special devotions are to be offered by those who are to be disciples of the shaykh following the manner prescribed by him.

To acquire the religious knowledge certain books are to be studied, such as faza'il namaz, faza'il Quran, faz'il zikr, faza'il ramazan, faza'il hajj, faza'ilsadakaat, and hikayat-i-sahaba. These books are in Urdu and are meant for Muslims in general. For the 'ulama' various sections from Sahih-al Bukhari are prescribed: *'kitab al-iman* (book of faith), *kitab al-ilm*(book of knowledge*), al-itisam* *bil-kitab wa al-sunnah* (adherence to Quran and the Practice of the Prophet), *kitab al-jihad* (book of struggle), *al-amr bill-maruf wa al-nahi 'an-al munkar, kitab al-adab, kitab al-riqaq and kitab al-fitan* (Haq, 1972).

The details of this divine command, its correct procedures are needed to be learnt through the learned scholars of religion. Usually, three procedures are to be adopted to get this particular aspiration of 'acquiring knowledge'. These are:

(a) By making urge for knowledge to other faithful Muslim brothers especially the ulama.

(b) By making self-efforts to acquire it, and;

(c) By prostrating before God or seeking Allah's help for the achievement of this goal.

Besides the Quran and Sunnah (hadith), relevant books as described above are believed to be a great source of knowledge. The contents are to be acquired and installed in the heart to mean that the knowledge is really acquired. Mere reading, understanding or its memorizing does not carry any merit. The knowledge in true sense is one that is conveyed by the creator of the universe through His messenger for the guidance of mankind, which is revealed in the divine books of Quran and Hadith. The knowledge has got importance and so is honoured. Ignorance has got no value and can bear no fruit. Knowledge alone is going to be useful in the grave and ignorance can never. Only those who acquired knowledge and acted upon will be able to pass through various trials and tests in the grave or on the Day of Judgment and thus will be able to shield or free themselves from the hellfire. Ignorance, or even knowledge with weak belief, or without compliance too will prove useless. The lives of the Prophet and his companions are the model for the Muslims about acquiring knowledge and acting upon (ibid).

- (4). **Respecting Muslims.** To pay due respect to the Muslims is called 'Ikram-e-Muslim' in Tablighi terminology, forms the next important principle of the Tablighi project. Maulana Ilyas emphasized that honour and deference should be shown to fellow Muslims, especially in the matter of rights. In addition to this, it is the special right of the young to be treated with affection by the elders, while elders are to be shown deference by the younger generation. At the same time Maulana Ilyas emphasized that rights are only a means to an end, the end being the spread of Islam. In the pursuit of this goal, one should be prepared to sacrifice one's own rights, for which one will be rewarded in the hereafter.

Thus, 'Ikram-i-Muslim' also stands for respecting others rights and not insisting ours. We should invariably fulfil the obligations towards other human beings as commanded by Allah, and as taught by Prophet Muhammad. We should do this task as a duty and should never demand our own right upon them. It should be our effort to serve others, in whatever way it is possible. Besides, it should be always our concern not to become a cause of trouble or problem for others. The poor needy, neighbour, should be taken care of. The elders, scholars, pious, should be looked with due regards. The weak, young and poor should be treated with compassion. We should overlook the weakness of others if we happen to come across. Allah will overlook our weakness on the Day of Judgment. We should understand the worth of our faithful Muslim brothers. It is reported in a Hadith, that Allah will continue to sustain the universe till that day all the faithful are dead. So Muslims are very dear to Almighty Allah. We find all the infighting; quarrels a today are because people generally enforce their rights on others and forget their duties towards them. It is the main cause of the quarrels and broken family bonds all around in the society now-days. We should volunteer ourselves for serving our brethren, the needy. The prophet Muhamad and his companions have a set of the excellent sacrifice of self-interest for us to replicate. It is narrated that once the Prophet had set on a tour along with the companions. On the way, they made a halt for a while for lunch. While others were busy in cooking, Prophet volunteered himself to collect the firewood. He has thus show-cased an excellent example of fraternity, service and social work. He always behaved one among the many. While in Jamaat or 'tablighi tour' one should to aside his 'individual' identity, status and act as one among the participants and act for the welfare of others (ibid).

The other aspect of this fourth principle is *akhlaque* meaning 'character building and imbibing moral values' and *haquq-ul-ibaad* meaning 'rights of the human beings' encompassing rights of the Muslims as well as mankind. It is through these moral values, character building and showing sympathy to Muslims and non Muslims like poor, sick, elderly and other needy Islamic teachings could be practically disseminated (Zainuddin 2020).

- (5). **Purity or sincerity of intention**. The fifth, important principle also called 'ikhlasi- niyyat'- in Tablighi parlance is concerned with emendation of intention and sincerity. Every action is to be undertaken with no other end in view but to please God Almighty Allah and to reform oneself. Any slightest deviation from this set path is bound to generate the wrath, anger of Allah instead as it tantamount to admitting partner in that deed. According to one hadith, a religious scholar, a philanthropist and a crusader will be brought before Almighty Allah on the Day of Judgment. They will be asked one by one to explain their behavior in the life. They will happily report about their performances and achievements. Allah will declare that their acts were with the intention to gain publicity and fame. It was achieved and nothing remains for them as a reward. They will be then ordered to be thrown in the fire of hell. It is also said that one of the attributes of Allah is being 'Pure' and He accepts only such deeds which are offered purely with an intention to gain His pleasure only. Hence the Muslims or the tabligi activists must ensure 'perfect purity in intention' is achieved at all costs. An impure act is dangerous and a way definite towards hell. A small act with purity in intention is great, considered acceptable and fully reward-able by Allah compared to a big one but with the slightest corruption in intention (ibid).

- (6) **Sparing time in the path of Allah. Or missionary tours.** Also called 'tafrigh-i- waqt' in tablighi terminology, means to spare time, i.e., to withdraw from one's worldly engagements and to go forth in missionary groups. This sixth principle 'making people come out of their homes' is central to the Maulana Ilyas's way of working because this gives people the opportunity to quit their worldly atmosphere and to go in search of the religious one. Only in an atmosphere free of worldly thoughts can be there a true receptivity to the message concerned. Ilyas is reported to have once said, 'our method of working, lays emphasis upon taking people out of their homes in groups. The main advantage of this method is to encourage people to come out of the worldly and static atmosphere to enter a new, pure and dynamic one where there is much to foster the growth of the religious consciousness. Besides, travel and emigration involve hardship, sacrifice and self-abnegation for the sake of Gods cause, and thus entitle one to divine succor (Khan, 1986:29).

This principle has also been referred to as 'the course of action' in the Tablighi literature because this is the principle where Muslims or tablighi activists are practically taught the above five principles. Thus this principle may be described as the essence or soul of tablighi project. While at his own place, one should move to bring people together for *salah* 'prayer', remembrance or *zikr* etc., in the local mosque. The fellow Muslim brothers should be argued to assemble in the evening and to stay back in the mosque to offer late-night salah 'prayer' called 'tahajud'. Supplication for forgiveness', guidance for all should be made to Almighty with a humble and begging posture. Again by persuasion, a jamaat should be formed to move out for three days to a nearby place. Some seniors should brief the junior participants the correct procedure of spending the time while in the path of Allah. A senior, learned among the group will be selected to head them to be called 'Ameer' of the group. The other important persons are the 'Mutakalim' i.e. a talk-giver and, a

'Rahbar' i.e. a guide- a local person of a village or an area where the Tableeghi Jamaat visits. A 24-hour program is prepared every day in the morning to practice to bringing of the 'six principles' in the lives of the participants. For this, the prescribed books are also read and recited while in the jamaat. The Muslims living in the village or around the mosque are contacted and invited, with an urge to join the jamaat and follow the same procedures for the success. This is done through the 'ghast' ie. Tablighi activists patrol in the locality around the mosque and went door to door or house to house while inviting people to mosque. The patrolling usually lasts for an hour, and the tablighi activists must return before 5 to 10 minutes before the salah (prayer). After salah, the 'Mutakalim' delivers speech or talk in a simple manner in the light of six principles to enlighten about the need of strengthening the bond of Muslims with the God-Allah. After this, a call is given by the 'ameer' usually in a gathering called 'tashkeel' [30] to the local people, to join the jamaat. Upon joining by some local people, similar groups numbering from 3-11 are formed there and dispatched to other places to work on the same pattern, for a convenient period. i.e. 3 days, 10 days, 40 days, 4 months etc. The dos and don'ts supposed to be observed while in the path are learnt from the seniors (Kandhalavi, 2009).

Thus, 'sixth principle' of the movement deals with the formation of the groups, of the volunteers, willing to donate their time for preaching tours. It advocates that it is the duty of every member of the community to call others to religion, just as in the past it had been the preoccupation of those who had accepted Islam upon the hand of the Prophet (Haq, 1972: 145).

These six positive (Haq, 1972) and fundamental principles are to be observed constantly by the members of the touring group. The **seventh essential principle** or rule is of prohibitive nature. This principle in tablighi parlance is called ***"Tarq-i-La'ya'ni"*** meaning, 'giving up useless actions or deeds'. This principle calls upon the Muslims or tablighi activists to abstain from wasting time in unnecessary talks, futile actions, sinful and prohibitive deeds. Besides these six principles (including the seventh) can be condensed into three main tenets:

'The 'Kalimah Tauhid', prayers and sparing time for preaching or good works. The other three are, in actual fact, offshoots of the main tenets. When they are adopted wholeheartedly all other things follow in consequence (Khan, 1986). And, when one 'spares time', in tabligi tours, he in the due course of time, learns by default about the other principles of the Jamaat. Besides, one must note that these 'tablighi' mobile units are not just formed to preach among people, but fundamentally to learn about Islam in the light of above mentioned six principles. So in the Tableeghi Jamaat, the members both learn and practice these six principles.

The above-mentioned six principles form the backbone of Tablighi Jamaat's *dawah* project encompassing its ideology and methodology. The first principle that is, *Kalima* profession of faith is the fundamental of all, all other principles follow logically and consistently. If one believes whole heartedly in Allah the way taught by Prophet Mohammad (PBUH), it is natural he will pray regularly, remember and praise Allah always, show respect to Muslims and mankind, spare time for learning and preaching Islam for the sake of Allah alone. However, the other distinguishing characteristic of Tablighi Jamaat's ideology and methodology is its fifth principle, *Tafrigh-i- waqt* that is, sparing time in touring and patrolling from one place to another place or from one mosque to another mosque while learning and practicing the Islam which also includes the learning of rest of the principles and their injunctions. It is primarily this principle of preaching methodology '*Tafrigh-i- waqt* (touring, travelling and patrolling), which distinguishes Tablighi Jamaat from other Islamic revival movements. Moreover, each and every Tablighi activist is strictly advised to abide by these principles both in the Jamaat as well as in his personal life. In nut shell, Tablighi Jamaat's core ideology in its present form is confined to these six principles (basic rituals) and unlike Jamaati Islami does not have any explicit and elaborate social, political and economic agenda.

TRANSLATION OF MAULANA SAAD'S SPEECH AND IDEOLOGY OF TABLEEGHI JAMAAT [31]

Translation of Maulana Saad's (Global leader of TJ also called Hazrat Ji) Speech entitled, *'Munkar Se Roukne Ka Fareeza'(Responsibility to Stop from Bad Deeds), while on a three-day trip (2019-20) to Global (Nizaam-ud-din- Delhi) Center of TJ.*

'one should bear in mind that the way or purpose of stopping from evil deeds is not to stop from evil deeds, which is not essential either but our purpose (TJ) is that 'munkir' or an evildoer should left/abandon that evil deed/s. The purpose is that one should abandon bad deeds, not to stop from them. The meaning of stopping bad deeds is that a man should come back from it.

Listen to me carefully! People think that unless until we don't go to 'munkir' (evil-doer) and stop him strictly from that evil, till our work is not done (of stopping him from evil); nonetheless the best way to stop anybody (evildoer) from evil is to make him aware of Allah, His mercy, His love, with love and compassion. It's in recognition of Allah, His love, His Mercy, that Allah has kept the power of stopping from evils.

A man's recognition (respect, love, gratitude) of an Allah is itself a way of keeping away from that evil. This is also because of the fact, that the sources or body parts which man uses in doing evils, he could use the same in recognizing Allah. If you bring him on that 'mauroofaat (recognition) of Allah His blessings), then there is no other best way than that. Also, because sometimes it becomes too difficult and uneasy for the evildoer to stop him of the evils, and instead he becomes more inclined towards wrongdoings. 'What would I say; we are living in the times when those involved in wrongdoings are accused, abused, charged and prosecuted? But the best way to keep away a wrongdoer from the bad deeds is to bring him/her out of the bad environment with love and compassion by realizing him/her about the blessings of Allah.

'The sources, means, power or efforts, which the 'Ummah' uses in stopping sins, I swear by Allah if only half of such efforts are spent in 'maroofaat' (introducing recognizing Allah and his blessings and love; Allah has with His creation), all the sins and bad deeds will vanish. Also, the sinner can't be prevented from sinning by accusing him, because the sinner is like one who has fallen in the pit. If you ask such a person that why he was not walking carefully and towards that side, would be like to kill him. Or if you merely give him/her an opinion or tactic to come out of the pit, would make no difference. As people say nowadays that our responsibility is only to provide ploy or opinion. If you only give ploy, I think such a person will not escape from the pit. The first and foremost trouble here is utilizing your resources to bring him out of the pit. In nutshell, its fact and quite essential to bring the wrongdoer from the bad environment towards the environment where he could recognize Allah His love and blessings. It's this which is the biggest source to bring an end to the evils'.

Concluding Remarks: This translation of Maulana Saad's speech highlights the basic approach, organizational strategy and ideology of TJ in its call towards Islam. As the main focus of TJ is on making Muslims good Muslims, this can be only done if they can be prevented from bad deeds and bad environment. So the focus is on bad deeds (evils), innovations and environment just like what was the focus of Ilyas in Mewat. Consequently, TJ invites people from this world /homely environment towards the *'Masjid'* environment. This case study also tells about TJ's aversion to mere opinions, readings and writings (publicity) and instead focuses on direct/ practical method of preaching. It also focuses on TJ's approach of humbling oneself before others while preaching and not on warnings or rude behaviour. Besides above it (Case Study), stresses on the 'maroofaat' i.e. on recognizing Allah (faith), His mercies and endless blessings, while giving the 'dawah for effectivity. It is because of this fact that Maulana Ilyas used to call it 'Tehreekh Imaan' (movement of the faith').

Footnotes

[5] Ummaha precisely refers to the believers or Muslims who believe in Prophet Muhammad (PBUH) as the last messenger of Allah. And broadly, it means all people (the whole of humanity) who came after Muhammad.

[6] Daw'at or dawah usually means invitation towards Islam, and tabligh means preaching, spreading the message of Islam.

[7] Muballig is an Urdu word for preacher.

[8] Shuddhi, is a Hindi word for purification,

[9] Nau-Muslims meaning Neo-Muslims.

[10]. Hadith means collection/record of the words, sayings or actions of the Prophet Muhammad.

[11]. According to Ilyas, Tablighi activists or Muslims must invite or present a message before Muslims in the light of six principles which form the crux of Ilyas's 'da'wah' (invitation) ideology. These six principles are discussed /given at the end of this chapter.

[12]. Bayaan refers to religious talk/preaching. for further see appendix III-B also.

[13]. Taleem means reading or recitation. In Tablighi parlance, it means reading the Quran or hadith or some scripts from Tablighi nisaab (books), while in preaching tours. For further see Appendix III- B

[14]. Purdah, specifically, means Islamic dress code for women, it also means covering or screening of women from men or strangers. However, broadly purdah does not mean just covering or screening of body, but also implies observing screening/ modesty, in talking, walking, and looking and applies to both men and women.

[15]. Nuh, is a district in Haryana.

[16]. https://purbanchal.blogspot.com/2010/04/tablighi-jamaat-in-mewat-part-3.html

[17]. https://purbanchal.blogspot.com/2010/04/tablighi-jamaat-in-mewat-part-3.html

[18]. http://twocircles.net/2010apr16/tablighi_jamaat_mewat_part_2.html

[19].   http://twocircles.net/2010apr16/
tablighi_jamaat_mewat_part_2.html

[20].   http://twocircles.net/2010apr16/
tablighi_jamaat_mewat_part_2.html

[21]. Ilyas is reported to have said, that how come one can claim that he is founding a jamaat when the jamaat of the believers has already been founded by Prophet Muhammad- for which constitution is based on the Quran, Mosque for the day today activities with its centres in Mecca and Medina, prayers and fasts among its program's.And he would prefer to call his movement by the name *Tahreek Emaan*. (for details see Haq, Anwarul: 45)

[22]. Ijtihad, means the use of individual intellect or 'independent reasoning, in applying Islamic law to the problems and concerns of modernity.

[23]. For details see Yoginder Sikand (1986) p.6-9, 72.

[24]. Sima means hearing music to bring about ecstasy, prevalent in some Sufi orders

[25]. Zikr or utterances of Allah, which are read or recited aloud

[26]. Kafir denotes 'atheist' or one who does not believe in one God or Allah and His Messenger Muhammad.

[27]. Praises of God-Allah; counting of beads one hundred times; rosary

[28]. Darood simply means paying salutation to Prophet Muhammad.

[29]. "istighafaar" is the act of seeking forgiveness from Allah, by reciting the Arabic word *Astaghfirullah*, repeatedly meaning "I seek forgiveness from Allah". Various other dua's are also recited for this purpose. It is considered one of the essential parts of worship in Islam.

[30]. Tashkeel, literally means 'put in pictures, practice, action or words' In Tablighi parlance, it refers to a special call on the part of the head or ameer of the tabligi jamaat to the local people about joining the tablighi tour for specific periods of time, usually 3, 7,10,40 (one chillah), and 120 days. Those accept the call, either raise their hands, or stand up, to register their names as per their

convenience. The names are written by one of the Tablighi members on the dairy. The registered people are contacted and departed for Tablighi tours, for various places.

[31]. This case study is my translation of Maulana Saad's (global head of TJ), speech which I recorded while I was on a three-day trip to Nizamuddin Dehli (global headquarters) centre of TJ (2019-20).

CHAPTER III

TABLIGHI JAMAAT: ORGANISATIONAL STRUCTURE

Tablighi Jamaat is one of the largest Islamic revival movements in the world. It is said to have a presence in about 200 countries with roughly about 200 million adherents throughout the world. Its annual gatherings are the largest next only after the hajj. This global presence and worldwide adherents are primarily because of its unique, loose, and free-flow organizational structure. In its organizational setup, it's fundamental for each member of the organization to play certain roles, duties, and responsibilities. These roles are played at the local, village, block/regional, district, state, and international levels. The membership of the organization is open to all Sunni Muslims, irrespective of the '*madhab*' or school of '*fiqh*' they belong to. A detailed discussion of the 'organizational structure' of the 'Tablighi Jamaat is given below in the following pages.

Tablighi Jamaat is a vague collection of loosely aligned, roving '*jamaats*' on the one hand; on the other hand, there is a fixed, hierarchical network of elders and mosques. About its loose fluid nature, Sardar writes, 'many South Asian Muslims living in the west, found themselves sinking into the activities of the 'Tableeghi Jamaat'one or the other day. Some of them become committed members of the 'jamaat' while many do not' (Sardar, 2004). Any Sunni Muslim could join the activities of the 'Tableeghi Jamaat'for a given period of time without having to be a committed Tableeghi. They may leave the organization whenever they wish or at a time of their liking (Pieri, 2015). Thus the membership of the organization is open to all. Any Sunni Muslim can join freely with the members or activities of the 'Tablighi Jamaat; he may stay for a long time or may leave the group at any time. So there is no restriction in joining and leaving the group. Any Muslim, all of whom are 'Sunni' can join the activities or be a member of the 'Tableeghi Jamaat' irrespective of the school of thought, 'fiqh' or jurisprudence they belong to (Y. Sikand, 2002).

The organization and structure of the 'Tablighi Jamaat' may be analyzed at both permanent and temporary levels. The permanent include the official leadership and hierarchies as well as level of prominence ascribed to each 'Tableeghi'– affiliated mosques and centres. The temporary level includes the composition of individual 'jamaats' that are sent out on missionary tours. The two are closely related (Pieri, 2015: 49-64).

About its fixed, centralized and hierarchical character, Goborieu (1992:21) comments that 'Tableeghi Jama'at' has from the very beginning remained, 'centralized and the leadership jealously kept by the lineage of the founder. Consequently, till today we found that leadership has remained among the descendants of the same family who founded it. Likewise, Mumtaz Ahmad (Ahmad, 1991) (1994:514) writes; 'the founder of the movement, that is 'Maulana Muhammed Ilyas Kandhalvi' was the first 'Ameer'(head) of the movement, which was followed by his son namely 'Maulana Mohammad Yusuf Kandhalvi' and the third 'Ameer'of the movement was Maulana Inam-ul Hassan.

Similarly, Yoginder Sikand (2002:81) writes; "after the demise of the 'Tablighi Jamaat's third leader, that is, Inamul Hassan in 1995, the leadership of the Jamaat was taken over by a 'Shoora'(consultative committee) comprising of three persons namely Izhar-ul Hassan (uncle of Maulana Ilyas), Sad-ul Hassan (son of Maulana Yousuf) and Maulana Zubair-ul Hassan (son of Inaam-ul Hassan). They continued to play an important role in the leadership of the 'jamaat.' However, it appears that before his demise in 1995, Maulana Inamul Hassan had constituted a 'Shura' of 'ten members' to look after the leadership of the 'jamaat.' The names of the members constituting the 'Shora' were: (1). Mufti Zainul Abideen, (2). Maulana Izharul Hassan, (3). Maulana Saed Ahmad Khan, (4). Maulana Umar Palanpuri, 5). Haji Abdul Wahab,

6). Maulana Zubairul Hassan, 7). Miyaji Mehraab, 8). Haji Afzal, (9). Haji Abdul Muqeet(engineer), and (10). Maulana Muhammad Saad Kandlalvi (the son of Maulana Mohammad Yousuf Khandalwi). [32]

After the death of Maulana Zubair-ul Hassan in 2014, conflict grew among the leadership of the 'jamaat,' which finally pavedthe way for their split in 2017. It appears, after the demise of Zubair-ul Hassan, Maulana Saad claimed to be the 'Ameer'of the Jamaatwhich was rejected by the Maulana Zuhair-ul Hassan (son of the Maulana Zubair-ul Hassan), and instead, he himself claimed to be the 'Ameer'of the Jamaat. This led to the formation of two rival groups among the leadership of the organization. One group was constituted by Maulana Saad and his followers, and the other group was comprised of Maulana Zuhair-ul Hassan and his followers [33]. In order to overcome this conflict and for the smooth functioning of the organization, a meeting was held in November 2015 by senior members of the 'Jamaat' from many nations. It was maintained that the 'shoora' established by Enam-ul Hassan- popularly called 'Hazrat Ji' need to be reconstituted in order to work on the same methodology or 'manhaaj' on which the previous three elders (akabeer) were working. Besides, the eight members of the previous 'shoora' founded by Maulana Enam-ul Hassan were already dead; thus 'Shora' was reconstituted to look after the various matters of the organization, especially pertaining to leadership, and to that of additions or corrections to it or the organization. After various opinions, discussions, and debates, a 'Shoora' of thirteen members were finally formed. This 'Shoora' is also called 'Aalmi Shoora' and is said to be formed in November 2015 after the yearly 'Raiwaind' 'ijtima' (gathering). The members comprising the 'Shora' are (1) Maulana Ibrahim Dewla (2) Haji Abdul Wahab, (3) Maulana Yaqoob, (4) Maulana Mohammad Saad, (5) Maulana Abdur Rahman, (6) Maulana Zuhair-ul Hassan, (7) Maulana Ahmed Laat, (8) Qari Zubair Sahab, (9) Maulana Nazr-ur Rehman, ((10) Maulana Rabaul Haq, (11) Maulana Ubaidullah Khursheed, (12) Bhai Wasif-ul Islam, and (13) Maulana Zia-ul Haq.

In the absence of any 'member' or members of the 'Shoora' by any reason like demise, it was decided that the gap would be filled through the consensus of the two-thirds majority of the Shoura. The *'shoora'* was also constituted to ensure the collectivity, particularly among the Nizamuddin (Delhi), Raiwand (Pakistan), and Kakarial centres of the 'Tablighi Jamaat.'[34]

However, the rift grew among the organizations and its followers throughout the world after the demise of Maulana Zubair-ul Hassan in 2014, primarily because of the self-proclaimed call of being 'Ameer'of the 'Tablighi Jamaat' by Maulana Mohammad Saad, without the consultation of the 'Shoura.' This rift gained public attention when intense clashes were reported to form the 'global' *Markaz* (meeting place /headquarters) of the 'Tablighi Jamaat' in 2017 between the two rival groups led by the Maulana Saad, and Zuhair-ul Hassan. These clashes at the 'global headquarters' were followed by intense clashes and conflict between the rival groups at other global centres like Bangladesh [35] and the United Kingdom. The controversial statements of Maulana Saad against the Quran and Sunnah and his rejection of the 'Shoora' are stated to be the root cause of conflict and the internal rift within the organization [36]. Consequently, these controversial statements and rejection of the Aaalmi Shora' also led to the clashes among the two camps of the Jamaat in 'Kakrial'- Bangladeshi headquarters on the one hand, and; on the other side, similar sort of clashes was witnessed among the two rival campuses, in the UK chapter of the 'Jamaat.' Some call this division is between the Nizamuddin Centre at the one hand, headed by Maulana Saad and Raiwand (Pakistan centre) on the other, looked and headed by 'thirteen members' 'Aalmi Shoora.' The constitution of 'Aalmi Shoora' in 2015 is said to have provided the platform to the opponents of the Maulana Sa'ad in 'Nizamuddin' headquarters and elsewhere in the world. In all, we can say that 'Tableeghi Jamaat' leadership and the organization has been divided into two rival groups worldwide: one group comprised of Maulana Sa'ad and his supporters, and; the other group comprised of 'Aalmi Shora' and their supporters. This organizational split into two groups deeply hurt the sentiments of the Tablieeghi followers all over the world and resulted in the creation of another 'third' group—the group comprised of people in deep shock, frustrated, and in a confused state of affairs. Likewise, the Pakistani Newspaper 'Dawn' under the heading 'A house Divided' on February 25, 2018, while reporting a British 'Tableeghi' volunteer saying, 'there are those who support Maulana Sa'ad Kanhalwi and 'Nizamuddin,' and there are others who oppose him, hence follow 'Aalmi Shoora.' But there is a third group or camp, comprising people like me (the British Volunteer), who are in an utterly confused state of affairs'[37]

In spite of the split, 'Tablighi Jamaat' continues to maintain a loose organizational structure and does not require any 'paid staff' or formal bureaucracy. The Maulana Ilyas is heard to be once said that "we have no party, no formal type of organization, no office, no register, no records, and no funds. Our work is to be shared by all Muslims. That is why, according to the times, we have not formed our people into a separate Jama'at (party). We are just working on the pattern of the mosques where people come together from different walks of life and, after having said their prayers, return to their daily chores. In the same manner, we ask you to spare some time to train yourselves and then go back to your daily activities" (Khan, 1986). The organizational work is largely carried out by small units of groups, who tour and travel from place to place and Mosque to Mosque. In each place, they usually reside in the mosque and go door to door to invite the people towards the mosque and present their message of da'wah in the light of the six principles. The strength of these little organizational groups varies between three to eleven members. The fundamental structure of these touring groups is that it contains at least three types of people having different roles and responsibilities. These are:

- (a). **'Ameer'or leader**: An 'Ameer' is a leader or head of the group. He is usually the most learned and senior member of the group. Amir's or heads of these roving 'Tableeghi' groups are appointed in the local *'markaz'* of the group by senior members heading the local *'markaz'*. He appoints the 'speaker', looks after the group's activities, and assigns various tasks, roles and responsibilities to the members of the group. It's the 'Sunnah' and duty of each *'Tableeghi'* member in the group to obey the decisions and orders of the 'Ameer.' Thus, the 'Ameer'provides leadership of the group.

- (b). **'Mutakalim' or speaker**. Speaker is a person who invites or presents talk before the people while patrolling or going door to door in the locality where the 'Tableeghi Jamaat' has visited. Speaker is also a person who gives talks to the gathering group or people in the mosque who have been invited, including the members of the 'roving' 'Tableeghi' group. The speaker's talk should be simple and direct. At any rate, it should not be too elaborate. The speaker is appointed by the 'Ameer.

- (c). **'Rahbar'or guide**. A guide is usually a local person who guides and leads 'the touring Tableeghi groups while going house to house and through the ways and streets of the area. In other words, his work is to show the 'paths' or various ways of the area, including the ones leading to residential houses. He also informs and introduces the arrival of 'Tableeghi' groups to the families of the residential houses of the area.

Besides the above-mentioned fundamental organizational structure, when the strength of the touring group is large, we find 'another group' rather 'fourth' group of members within the organization called *'khadim'* (the ones who serve).

- (d). **'Khadim'** (which means the 'one who serves). In most cases, this group is always present within the preaching group. The strength of the group usually varies from one to three members. Their work is to prepare the food and serve it to members of the group. They also visit the market and shop for the group, in particular concerning the foods and dishes they prepare for the group. In other words, *'khadim'* is a person or group of people who make arrangements for the food for the 'Tableeghi Jamaat.' They cook food and prepare certain dishes, bring vegetables, fruits, wheat, rice, etc., from the market, clean utensils, and serve food to the preaching group. They are also called the group associated with the *'khidmat'* meaning 'serving.' They are appointed by the *'Ameer.'*

Likewise, regarding the fundamental structure of the preaching group, M.S. Agwani writes, 'a tableeghi' preaching team must have an 'Ameer'(head or leader), *muttakallim* (speaker), and a *'rehbar'* (guide). The size of the team varies between a minimum of three and a maximum of ten members. An average team must contain both the learners and instructors. Though indeed, 'Ameer' provides the leadership of the group, however, he must listen, consult, and look after the requirements of his colleagues. Besides, he must give the opportunity to speak to everybody regarding the matters pertaining to *'tabligh'* and must instil in them good manners like religiosity and modesty. The 'Ameer' may speak himself, or he may appoint 'a a speaker' to address the people. The work of the speaker is to invite the local Muslims of the target area, in the most humble and convincing manner, towards the faith or fundamentals of Islam. And, if the speaker, while talking or addressing the people of the target area, commits any mistake, then it was the responsibility of the 'Ameer' to correct the 'speaker' in the most responsible and judicious manner. However, the main emphasis of the 'speaker' was to be on instructing people, including the members, about how to do ritual prayers and read the 'Quran' correctly. Among the members, those who learned should concentrate on teaching, and those who 'do not' should concentrate on learning. So far as the 'guide' is concerned, his work was associated with some practical arrangements, such as cooking, travel, and other associated chores (Agwani, 1986).

Besides, 'Tablighi Jamaat' members do not get any wages or any payments while going door to door, or Mosque to Mosque, while in the preaching tour. They finance themselves for their entire burden, and all the members spent their own money while in the 'jamaat.' Maulana Ilyas was also against the donations donated to the group. He believed that the 'da'wah' or work of Islam could be promoted only by participating in the 'Tableeghi'tours and not by donating any money. Thus, he laid it down as a 'rule' that each 'Tablighi member' of the roving missionary group must pay for all his travel, food, and other requirements (Agwani, 1986: 43). Haji Abdul Wahab- head of the 'Tableeghi Jamaat' chapter Raiwind headquarters- Pakistan, was donated a huge amount by some Pakistani Politician, but he rejected the offer and instead requested his time and not the money. To the query raised by the politician, 'that nobody could donate you such a large amount,' Abdul Wahab is said to have replied that 'everybody cannot object to such a huge amount.' Thus 'Tablighi Jamaat' dislikes donating money and occasionally accepts only from the regular, devoted, and senior members of the 'Tabligh'(Putra, 2013). Thus, overall, we can say that 'Tableeghi Jamaat activists meet their all expenses by themselves while in the preaching tour.

While in the 'Jamaat,' the activists or 'preaching tours' are usually 'organized' in four ways on the basis of the duration spent in the tour. These are; 'one day in a week, 'three days in a month, 'forty days in a year, and three 'chillahs' or 'one hundred twenty days' once in a year. This strategy for the organizational work was evolved by Ilyas himself. Likewise, Anwarul Haq mentions that Maulana Ilyas strictly required from the members of the 'Tabligh movement' that;

- (i). They should preach 'every week' in their own locality.
- (ii). They should go to nearby villages for three days every month, within a distance of 'five' kilometres.
- (iii). That they should spend at least one *chillah* (forty days) in a year for da'wah, and,
- (iv). That they should leave their homes at least for 'four months' once in one's lifetime for the learning and preaching of Islam (Haq, 1972).

However, Maulana Mohamad Yosuf Kandhalwi (second head of the Jamaat), increased it to six months in a year and asked people to devote their entire life to the work of teaching (ibid).

Tablighi Jamaat does not contain any literature or office records that may be said to contain the 'official position' of the 'Jama'at' regarding its membership or activities. Maulana Ilyas has rightly put it, 'we have not formed any separate party, for our work is to be shared by all Muslims. Thus we have no records, no office, no formal organization, no funds, and no register' (Khan, 1986). Likewise, Mumtaz Ahmad is of the view that "the dawah methodology of the Jamaat by it is very nature is predisposed to expansion rather than consolidation or organization building and has mitigated against the usual processes of institutionalization and bureaucratization which so characterize the Jamaat-i-Islami. After more than sixty years of its existence, the 'Tableeghi Jamaat'remains a free-floating and informal association with no full-time works, no elaborate office records, no division of labour, and no institutional network of functional departments and branches. There are no formal decision-making procedures. In fact, decisions are sometimes made on the basis of dreams and *'basharat'* (inspirations) (Ahmad, 1991). They believe Islam is not something to be written, talked, paying lip service or read about, but a 'practical work' (*amaali kaam),* which must be attained, struggled and followed practically. As Yoginder Sikand, puts it, while reporting, the British 'tableeghi' member saying, 'our motto is no *'charcha'* (publicity), no *'parcha'* (records or literature) and no *'kharcha'* (donations or expenditure). They seek intentionally low, introvert organizational profile believing that publicity and western means of communication affects spirituality and divert ones attention from 'fundamental' to irrelevant or incidental things. However, in the later years of life, after the success of the movement, Ilyas is heard to have said that 'there was no need to stick to the old method and now 'tableeghi' leaders or members should write as much as they can.' Consequently, nowadays, there are many slim tract books available in the market about the

'Tableeghi Jamaat'; however, they continuously show an aversion to publicity and worldly fame. Besides, they are of the view that it's 'Sunnah' and the tradition of 'Sahaba' to preach directly; thus, they also advocate for the direct, personal, and oral method of preaching. Additionally, they are also of the view that personal communication is far better than indirect communication over books or media, for it allows us to understand the target 'people' very well. We can modify our approach as per the needs, understandings, temperaments, and aspirations (Zainuddin, 2006; Sikand, 2002; W. Khan, 1986; Tariq, 1995).

The organizations' activities of the Tableeghi Jamaat are coordinated through centres and headquarters called *'markaz'* an 'Arabic term meaning 'centre', thus denoting central meeting place. Tableeghi Jamaat maintains its *'marakaz's* or headquarters at international, national, regional or local levels.

Global or International Level

The global or international headquarters *'aalmi markaz'* of the 'Tableeghi Jamaat' is located in South New Delhi, India, in the locality of Basti Hazrat-i-Nizamuddin. The headquarters are located in the multi-floor building, which consists of an Islamic seminary also called the 'Kashf-ul Uloom', a mosque called 'Bangli Wali Masjid', and many halls and rooms for the visitors and the guests.

This global 'centre' or headquarter of the 'Tableeghi Jamaat' is commonly called 'Nizamuddin Markaz' or Nizamuudin Center. The name of the 'centre' has been named after a great Islamic Preacher, Hazrat Nizamuddin Aulia, whose tomb is located near the 'Bangle Wali Masjid.'

This global headquarter is also the residential place of various elders or *'buzzargaan'* of the movement, residing in their own small cells. This 'global *markaz*' owes much importance to the movement. It is a place where the movement was formally launched from 'Bangle Wali Masjid' and also where the founders, pious predecessors, or 'ameers' (heads) of the movement are buried. Till 1995, the global headquarters were presided over by a single 'ameer', who was elected for life by a council of elders. Maulana

Enam-ul Hassan was the last or 'third' such 'Ameer'or head of the movement who died in 1995. After his death, the leadership was transferred to a consultative committee also called 'Shora' consisting of three persons, Izhar-ul Hassan (uncle of Maulana Ilyas), Muhammad Zubair-ul Hassan (son of Enam-ul Hassan), and Sa'ad-ul Hassan (son of Maulana Yousuf). They were further served and helped by a group of 'fifty workers' and a team of 'twenty seniors' who were each responsible for various tasks (Y. S. Sikand, 1998) Durani 1993:24). However, after the death of the Zubair-ul Hassan in 2014, the 'Shoora' of three members (or 'ten members') formed by Enam-ul Hassan was reconstituted in 2015, and 'thirteen' member new consultative committee or 'Shora' was formed, consisting of Ibrahim Dewla, Maulana Saad, Haji Abdul Wahab, Maulana Abdur Rahman, Maulana Yaqoob, Maulana Ahmad Laat, Mualan Zuhair-ul Hassan, Qari Zubair Sahab, Maulana Rab-ul Haq, Maulana Nazrur Rehman, Bhai Wasif-ul Islam Maulana Ubaidullah Khursheed, and Maulana Zia-ul Haq [38]. The 'Nizamuddin Markaz' is a hub of activities throughout the year. The 'Tableeghi Jamaat' members come here from all over the world, learning different activities, principles, and methods of the 'tabligh' from the local elders and mentors of the 'Jamaat'. The elders of these touring groups to 'global *markaz*' also report the progress and activities of the Jamaatfrom the respective countries or areas they had came from to the leaders stationed at the 'global *markaz*'. In turn, they receive some suggestions and instructions from them.

State or National Headquarters

Tablighi Jamaat maintains '*markaz*' or headquarters at the state or country level. These regional headquarters are mostly located in the capital cities of the countries. Usually, these 'regional' headquarters are located in the mosques having sympathy for the movement. The congregations in these mosques mostly consist of members either associated or sympathetic to the Jamaat. There is an 'Ameer'for each state, generally nominated by the authorities at the global or New Delhi '*markaz*'. The work of these state-level headquarters is to look after the activities and progress of the movement at the country level.

District/Town/Block/Local Level Headquarters

These headquarters look after the progress and activities of the movement at local levels. There may be a single or many headquarter(s) in a district or a town depending upon the population of the Muslims having membership or sympathetic to the group. There is also an 'Ameer'in each of these headquarters, generally appointed by the elders at the state level. These are the headquarters that provide the opportunity to learn and practice the 'dawa'ah' at the grass-roots level.'

However, in some countries, a significant shift was seen in the structure of 'Tablighi authority after the 1990s, with a single *'Ameer'* being replaced by a collective leadership, probably in an effort to stem factional rivalry (Y. Sikand, 2002).

The responsibilities of the *'markaz'* at various levels are both to encourage the Muslims to join the work of the movement as well as to coordinate 'jamaat activities' in their own areas. Thursday evenings and in some places Saturday evenings are usually set apart for the weekly gathering or *'ijtima'* in which a large number of people, including visiting activists from outside and local men, come to the *'markaz'* to listen to lectures delivered by experienced 'Tableeghi leaders or workers. These invariably focus on the pressing need for the Muslims to strengthen their faith, to strictly observe the Islamic rituals, to lead a pure, Islamic life, and to immerse themselves completely in the work of 'Tablighi Jamaat'. After speeches, members of the congregation are encouraged to register their names as participants in jamaats' going to different places at varying lengths of time.

The schedule of the 'jamaats' is usually carried out by the authorities or leadership at the local level, primarily in consultation with the leadership at the higher levels like district, national or international levels. However, at the state level other than India, the schedule of the 'jamaats' is carried out in consultation with the leadership at 'central *markaz*'. Then the leadership at various levels invite and assemble together all those who have voluntarily enlisted their names to participate in the roving 'jamaats' Their names are read aloud, and they are then asked to choose among themselves the *'ameeri jamaat'* or group leader. The groups are then dispatched on the 'dawah tour' to various places for a specific period under the leadership of the head or 'ameer-i jamaat'. When these travelling 'Tableeghi' groups come back from respective areas after a specific time, then they report to the local *markaz*. Here the leaders of these travelling groups or *'muballigeen'* at this local 'markaz' narrate the experiences or activities to the local leaders. Besides, they also give a detailed report about the progress of the organization in the respective places they have visited before the elders and leaders of the movement at the local level. In 'Tableeghi' terminology, this is called *'karguzari'* (see also appendix).

The 'Tableeghi' leadership at the 'local level' keeps constant with the leadership at higher levels like state, provincial or district levels. In turn, the leadership in each country at the central level or 'central *markaz*' keeps close links with the leadership of the 'Tableeghi Jamaat' at the global level located in New- Delhi, India. Regular reports about the progress of the 'Tableeghi movement' or its 'dawah' work are given to the elders stationed at 'global *markaz*'. In turn, they (leaders of each country) receive suggestions and instructions from the 'global leadership' from time to time. The association between these different 'levels of organizational structure' is further strengthened by regular tours of 'Tableeghi leadership'. On the one hand, leaders stationed at the global headquarters pay regular visits to different countries either to address huge gatherings or simply tour as participants' in the roving 'jamaats'; on the other hand, leadership at different levels pay regular visits to New Delhi 'global headquarters for the same purpose. However, the communication or the usual exchange of letters between the authorities at different levels of the organizational structure largely remains oral.

Taken as a whole, the method of engaging in 'Tablighi work'(*tariqa-i- tabligh*), as developed over time by Maulana Ilyas and his son Mohammad Yousuf, is almost in all respects, still faithfully followed by the 'Tableeghi Jamaat' members in all countries, where it is active. In fact, great stress is laid on the importance of strictly abiding by this method, for its claim, not only is this 'natural method' *(fitri tariqa)* but above all, the method, that the Prophet himself used *(nabavi tariqa)* (Sikand, 2002).

6.2 THREE-DAY ACCOUNT/ORGANISATIONAL STRUCTURE OF TABLIGHI JAMAAT [39]

"In the TJ many times I came across the words of various speakers, speaking to the members of the group that at least a three days 'jamaat' should be ready to form and go on the *'tabligh'* from a village after a one month of hard work through meetings/ appointments in that *'basti'* or village. When such 'Jamaat' will be formed for three days, it must have at least 5 to 6 members.

In this 'Jamaat' one will be 'Ameer' (head) and the rest *'mamoor'* over whom the head is appointed. The 'Ameer' should be an adult and possessing a wit. The best 'Ameer' is the one having the knowledge, and the best 'jamaat' is one having the 'hafiz'(one who has memorized the Quran) and *'aalim'* (scholar) in it. The 'Jamaat' departs from the 'masjid' of their *'basti'* to a nearby place; often, the neighbouring place is preferred. In the Masjid, the members are reminded/taught by the 'Ameer' that there are two intentions of joining the 'Tabligh viz. to learn and practice 'Deen', and second to preach it towards others. Before its departure, the members are taught various etiquettes of departure *(rawaangi k adaab)* viz. the mutual recognition of the head *(Ameer)* and the members *(mamoor)*, the group's required kinds of stuff (bag and baggage) which includes meal set, books, *fazail amaal* (part i and ii) and some clothes. The first thing which is told during the departure is that the 'jamaat' should follow 'Ameer' within the limits of 'Shariat'. Then comes the etiquettes of walking, which includes a prohibition on chatters/useless talks, walking in pairs, teaching and learning from each other whenever there is an opportunity, reciting 'zikr'/tasbbihaat' when there is no such opportunity, and walking on the side of the road. If there is a departure or travel through the bus, then one member is given the responsibility of keeping an eye on the luggage, and the one member takes the responsibility of fare. When the group reaches the target/neighbouring 'basti', they make dua/invocation to Allah about their acceptance in His way, including the target community, and seek the pleasure of Allah for themselves as well as for the community. On entering the neighbouring mosque, the 'Ameer' once again reminds them of the purpose of their coming to that village, i.e., they have come for their own guidance/learning and not to preach/advise others. Afterwards, 'Ameer' tells them about the 'etiquettes of mosque', which first of all includes telling them about the significance/importance of Masjid like that mosque is the house of Allah in which worldly talks, making noise, speaking loud and walking fast or running is strictly prohibited. Besides, one is also prohibited from going inside the mosque while using foul/dirty smelling foods like garlic, onion or cigarettes. Afterwards 'two rakaat (raka`h) prayer called 'Tahitul Masjid' is offered by all the members, after which they immediately assemble and join the 'mashwara [40]' (consultation/counselling). According to them there are blessings in the consultation, and members are told about its virtues (virtues of consultation). In the consultation, many things are determined like who will serve ('khidmat' [41] (service), who will educate/teach ('taleem' [42] (education), and; who will take the responsibility of meeting/s 'mulakaat' (meetings/appointments). In consultation, two members are appointed for 'khidmat', so that the group will not become a burden on others. For 'taleem' one member, preferably most educated/knowledgeable, is appointed. First of all, he educates/teaches the members about the virtues of the Quran. He then asks members to recite Quran (its various chapters) one by one. In this way, he helps them to learn, memorize, and recite it correctly. Afterwards, he reads and explains (wherever necessary) various parts of the 'fazil-amaal'. Besides, he also teaches and tells them about the six principles, 'chai sifaat'. The total time to be spent in the 'Taleem' in this morning session is two and a half hours.

After the 'taleem' comes *'mulakaat'*. For 'mulakaat' two members are appointed, who first of all meet with the 'Imaam' (one who leads the prayers) of the mosque and inform him about the coming of TJ in the mosque. Then they ask him about his advice and prayers. Next, they meet scholar/s and pious/religious personalities of that place in order to seek their advice, guidance, and prayers. This is called 'first mulakaat' (meeting) in 'Tablighi' parlance. It's done with the great religious personalities, in their terminology with *'deen kay badhe'* (Islam's great) personalities. After this first meet, *'mulakaat'* comes the second meeting *('dusri mulakaat'),* in which members of the TJ meet with leaders of the place, preferably the 'Masjid Committee'. They are being asked; that they are the responsible members of the community, who look after its various needs like electricity, water, etc. and, how 'Deen' is also important for its members. They are being asked/taught that if *'Deen'* will come to this *'basti'* or place, then Almighty Allah blesses it with various mercies. So they are humbly consulted and requested for their help in advising the people about the purpose of 'Jamaat's' visit to that place or *'basti'*. In 'Tabligi' parlance, 'second meeting' is done with *'Duniya k badey'* (translated as world's great), i.e., with leaders/great personalities of the place. After the 'second meeting' comes the third meeting, *'teesri mulakaat',* which is being done with those members of the place who have already spent some time with the TJ. These old members of the group are requested for their guidance by spending some time with them. However, it must be noted that these activities viz. *'khidmat' 'taleem'* and *'mulakaat'* are usually done simultaneously and not one after another. In most of the cases, *'taleem'* precedes, and these are subjected to certain conditions like availability of the respective resources.

After these, the members of TJ are taught about the etiquettes of eating. The members are being told that they should eat on the pattern of 'sunnah', and in the meantime, lunch is served. After lunch, the members are told to prepare immediately for the 'Zuhr' prayers. After the prayers, usually, the 'Ameer' gives a brief 'introductory bayaan' speech, in which he tells about the 'purpose of their visit and necessity of 'Deen' in their 'basti' or place. For instance, he tells them if they will follow Islam, then there will be peace, love, and brotherhood everywhere, and the 'doors of mercy' will be opened for them by Allah and the doors of doom closed. In this introductory lecture, he further asks them that 'Islam comes in existence through two things; first, through migration *'hijrat'* and second through help *'nusrat'*. In the first part (*hijrat*), the stories, struggles, and sacrifices of the Prophet in the way of Islam (dawah) are narrated/ (taught) like how He left even his home 'Makkah' and migrated to Medina, His journey of 'Tayiff' etc. In the second part, *'Nusrat,'* they are told that how Prophet and his companions were welcomed and helped in 'Medina'. So in this way, the people of the *'basti'* are told that they have too migrated in the way of Islam, and they are sure that they will be helped by them too (local people). At last, in this session, a call is given to members of the community to join the TJ, and the names of those ready to help or join the 'Jamaat' are registered. The total duration of this 'introductory speech' usually lasts between 10-20 minutes.

After this 'introductory speech,' the members of the TJ start participating in 'Second Taleem'. In this *'taleem'* 'Fazial Amaal' part, the second is read and taught for about half an hour. After *'taleem'* the members of the TJ talk, discuss and learn about the 'Sunnah's' (prophetic acts) and *'faraiz'* (obligatory acts) of ablution, bathing, and prayers. After *'taleem'* the members of the TJ take rest and practice 'Qailullah' or nap (short midday sleep), which according to them, is 'Sunnah' and very beneficial. After napping, the responsible members serve the tea by placing first a clean sheet or cloth (*dastarkha*) over the ground, around which the members of the group sit in two rows. Then on this cloth, the members place first bread over it, followed by teacups. After the tea is served, preparations for the 'Asr' prayer are made. Soon after the prayers, the next speech/talk/lecture *'bayaan'* starts, in which the stories and struggles of the prophets are narrated/taught to the people, including members primarily. After this talk, the members of the group are taught about the virtues of patrolling *'fazailli ghastt'*.

Afterwards, the members, minimum three and maximum ten, go for patrolling 'ghast' in the *'basti'*. In the meantime, one member is assigned the role of welcoming/receiving the people; the second is assigned the role of doing 'zikr' and praying for them' and the third one is assigned the role of speaking (religious talk) to them. In the patrolling group 'ghast jamaat', there is one guide, 'Rahbar,' one speaker, 'Mutakalim' and one leader "Ameer/zamidaar'. The work of the Guide 'Rahbar' is: to show ways (roads /streets /lanes/ passages) of the *'basti'*; to lead residential houses, to knock at the doors, to greet, to call with good names, and to cast down his eyes or glances. The work of the Speaker 'Mutakalim' is: to greet or shake hands with everyone he could meet, to talk about faith and hereafter, and to request to be present in the mosque. The work of the Head 'Ameer' is: to keep group concentrated with zikr; to admonish them of any negligence; to urge members to recite 'Third Article of Faith; and; if they are in market then to urge them to recite 'Fourth Article of Faith'. On the completion of the patrolling 'ghast' while returning, the members are urged to recite 'Istigafaar' (words of repentance/forgiveness).

After patrolling, 'Magrib Namaaz' is offered, immediately after which a general lecture 'ummomi bayaan' is started in the light of six principles. At the end of this lecture, members of the community are urged to join and register their names with the group. In this way, various groups are formed for three days, ten days, forty days, and four months. This is called *'tashkeel'* in 'Tablighi' terminology. However, much emphasis is not placed on the *'tashkeel'* as it is only the way of identifying the people desiring to join the 'Tabligh.' Instead, the emphasis is laid on the meetings *'mulakaat'* to make the groups whereby these people are personally met and convinced to join the 'Tabligh.' These meetings are held immediately after the completion of religious talk 'bayaan,' and if there is no time then these people are met on next day either in the 'Masjid' or by visiting their homes. After the religious talk (bayan) or these meetings, the preparations for the 'Isha Namaaz' are made. When the prayers are done, the members review the whole day from the standpoint of deeds and thus self-evaluate their work. In case if any member has forgotten any deed like reciting Quran or 'Zikr' he is then asked to repay/ re-compensate by doing that once again. Afterwards, members discuss and learn the etiquettes of eating and sleeping. Then the food is served (dinner), immediately after which preparations for sleeping are made so that all members could pray 'Tahajjud', whereby they could seek blessings for themselves, the community, and the whole 'Ummah'. Subsequently, 'Fajr Namaaz' is offered, after which religious talk *bayaan* starts in the light of six principles. Then the members pray 'Ishraaq', after which the breakfast is served by the responsible members. Soon after the breakfast, members assemble for Consultation 'Mashvara' (which has been discussed above).

The above schedule is followed for the second and third day also, and the rest of the days while TJ is on a *'dawah'* trip. However, after the return and completion of the three-day trip, the members are asked that they were in the religious setting (environment of the Masjid); and thus, it was easy for them to practice Islam. Now they will not get such settings or the environment in their locality. So they are asked to be steadfast on Islam, for which they are given some individual and collective tasks/responsibilities. In the former individual members are asked to strictly adhere to five times compulsory prayers, additional prayers, recitation of Quran, remembrance, and glorification of Allah ('zikr/ *tasbihaat'*) and to keep good/simple relations with people, especially of the community. Additionally, they are asked to live a simple life on the model of Prophet (PBUH) and to keep themselves away from showoff and other bad deeds. In the latter, members are advised to strictly adhere to consultation 'Mashvara' to draw out their plans on a daily basis. Here they are asked that they should arrange meetings and patrolling in the locality and neighbouring mosques and places at least twice a week. Besides, they are asked to practice 'Taleem' (learn /read Quran, Fazil-i-Amaal) both in *'Masjid'* and at home. Additionally, they are also told to visit once a week to local *'Markaz'* and to spend three days each month with the TJ.

This case study describes/highlights various things about the procedure of invitation and organizational activities of the TJ. For instance, TJ groups ranging from five to fifteen depart from a local mosque to the nearest place/mosque, while upon reaching, they meet some influential people (religious and worldly) in order to facilitate their religious revival program. It talks about that 'Ameer' should be followed by members *'mamoor'* only as long as he conforms to 'shariah.' Thus, it could be termed as a fundamentalist movement giving ultimate place to 'shariah' in its guidance to work. It also talks about various important concepts or strategies of TJ like *mutakalim, rahbar, mashvara, khidmat, ghast, mulakaat, taleem, tashkeel,* and *bayaan,* which hold an important position in the organizational work of the group. Besides the above, this case study probably tells us about everything the members of TJ do while they are in the 'Tabligh.'

ORGANISATIONAL ACTIVITIES AND STRATEGIES [43]

The various organizational activities and strategies which hold an important place in the organizational structure of the Tablighi Jamaat are discussed as follows:

- **A. Mashwarah or Mashvara.** Mashwara means consultation. There may be weekly and daily consultations between the leaders and members of Tablighi Jamaat. In its weekly Mashwara at the zonal mosque, an ameer (head) is appointed by the leaders at the zonal mosque for every Jamaat coming under its jurisdiction. In this weekly gathering, the rukh (direction of a place to be visited) is decided by the respective leaders of the zone, and thus jamaats are dispatched under the leadership of an ameer. Similarly, when Jamaat visits a village or place after praying an individual prayer called Tahitul Masjid, in a local mosque, they sit together to hold Mashwarah.

The Ameer instructs and explains the importance, virtues, necessity and various etiquettes of the Mashwara to all the members. Then the various roles are allocated to the members of the group.

- **B. Khidmat (service).** At the end of the consultation that is Mashwara, some members of the touring group are assigned the task of arranging, preparing, cooking and serving food to all the members of the group. This is called as 'Khidmat' in Tablighi terminology. Usually, two to four members are assigned these roles.

- **C. Elan (announcement).** In the consultation, one of the members of the travelling/preaching group is assigned the role of the announcement; that is, after the *namaaz* prayers,one of the members of the group gets up and announces about the arrival of that group in that *basti* locality or place. In the announcement, he requests all the people to stay after the prayers and to listen to the *deen ki baat* that is a religious talk or lecture given by one of the members after the prayers.

- **d. Taleem (Reading/reciting).** In Taleem, some passages from the books like Fazail Amaal and Muntakhib Ahadith are read out among the members of the group. All the members listen attentively, often sitting shoulder to shoulder with each other in a circular position. All the members are expected to remain in a state of *wadhu* (ritual purity/ablution) during this session. It is explained to the members that when people sit together in *taleem*, the angels surround these people, listen, note and inform Allah about this all programme. After this general session of reading the books for an hour, the Jamaat or group splits into two-three subgroups depending upon the strength of the Jamaat. In these subgroups, each and every member is taught to learn and recite some verses from the Quran, including Kalimah (article/profession of faith)

After this programme, all the members are taught and learned about the *chai batein* six principles of the Tableegh and their importance. Moreover, there are two sessions of the *taleem*, one is held after the *namaaz-e-zohr* (afternoon prayer) and the second after namaaz-e-Isha (late evening prayer). In this second session of the *taleem*, the stories of the Prophets and various companions of the Prophet Mohamad (PBUH), including the Prophet himself, are narrated to the members of the group. Mostly these stories are read out from the book, namely Hikayat-e-Sahaba. All the members listen attentively with devotion.

- **e. Ghast or patrolling.** Ghast holds much importance in the Tablighi Jamaat. It is one of the most fundamental characteristic techniques of TJ's Islamic revival project. It's primarily because of this technique it stands distinguished from other Islamist movements. Also, because of this feature, Khalid Masud aptly called TJ by the name 'Travelers in Faith' and wrote a basic book on them with the same title. It holds the most important position in the organizational work of TJ. So it is in this backdrop worthwhile to mention various types of patrolling in the case of TJ.

Patrolling in TJ's parlance is called as 'ghastt'. It is also referred as touring, migrating or travelling for the purpose of spreading Islam. There are mainly 'five types [44] of ghasts or patrolling in the Tableeghi Jamaat. These are:

1. **Khasoos-i -Gasht (Essential/Special ghast):** It is conducted when Tableegi Jamaat goes for 'dawah' to another place. This is called migration 'hijrat' or hijrah in Islam. According to the respondents, migration is fundamental rather than obligatory *'farz'* and a Prophetic tradition 'sunnah' for the establishment of Islam. According to them, Islam came into existence through two ways: one through migration 'hijrah when Prophet Mohammad (PBUH) migrated to Medina and second through assistance *'nusratt'* from the people of the Madina *'ansaar'* who helped Prophet (PBUH) in time of need. Thus when the group departs and reaches another place, they meet there three different types of people, immediately after the consultation

'mashwara': with the heads or high profile personalities of the place or *'basti'* (*duniya ka badey*), with the religious personalities including 'Ulama', Clerics, masjid 'Imaams' and with the native, former members of the TJ. This 'ghast' is called *'khasusi'* or essential 'ghast' and holds an important position in the organizational strategy of the TJ. The main purpose of this 'ghast' is to win the confidence of these people to facilitate their purpose or preaching of Islam.

2. **Taleem-i-Gasht (educational ghast):** It is performed during the time of *'taleem'* in Masjid. Some of the members are sent outside the mosque to invite anyone who could meet them outside for participating in the *'taleem'*. It is conducted for a short duration. Once any person meets them outside, they immediately come back to the mosque along with him to participate in *'taleem'* and then the Ameer select a few other members to do the same. This process continues until the *'taleem'* ends.

3. **Umoom-i-Gasht (general ghast):** After the 'khususi ghast' in which only a few special people are met, in general, 'gasht' all people of the place are met by going door to door to their houses. It is usually performed after 'Asr' (which is prayed before sunset) or Maghrib Namaaz. The Members go door to door among the Muslim community without any pick and choose to invite people to participate in the religious talk in Masjid.

4. **Tashkeel-i-Gasht:** It is conducted on a selective basis. The members go to the selected households where they meet the male members and give them *Dawah* (invitation), to spend some time in the way of Allah. In this 'gasht', the local members of the TJ help in the selection of individuals who they feel will join the TJ.

'Tashkeel' literally means 'put in pictures, practice, action or words'. It also means 'to form' or 'to organize'. Thus 'tashkeel' may be said as a process in which 'Tablighi' efforts are put into practice by forming the roving jamaats. (Zainuddin, 2000). In Tableeghi parlance, it refers to a special call on the part of the head or 'Ameer' of the Tableeghi Jamaat to the local people about joining the Tableeghi tour for specific periods of time, usually three, seven, ten, forty (one chillah), and 120 days. Usually, after the Magrib namaaz when the speaker completes his religious talk, he requests local people to spare some time with the TJ. The first call is given for four months or three chillas; the second call is given for forty days or one chillah, the third call is given for ten days, followed by other calls given for seven and three days, respectively. In each call, he persuades the local people to register their names. Those who accept the call either raise their hands or stand up to register their names as per their convenience. The names are written by one of the Tableeghi members on the dairy. The registered people are later contacted and departed for Tablighi tours for various places.

5. Wasooli Gasht: It is performed for those individuals of the place who have written their names with the TJ. Actually, in this 'ghast', those people are met, who have already written or registered their names for joining the TJ, at the time of 'tashkeel'. So either local volunteers of the TJ or more often 'Ameer' of the travelling group including 'rahbar' visit the homes of these individuals. On visiting, they are reminded and persuaded to join the TJ. The Tableeghi members collect some money from them for their eatery and other necessities, if they wish so in advance.

- **f. Bayaan (talk).** After completing the Ghast (patrolling) all the members of the group, including the residents, assemble in the mosque for offering namaaz. When the prayers are completed, then the *Mutakalim* or the speaker gives the *bayaan* or religious lecture to all people present in the mosque. The speaker is generally the experienced member of the group, and in most of cases, it is *Ameer* head of the group who gives a talk. The speech is expected to be simple, precise and persuasive. Utmost care is taken to avoid the tune of superiority or command over the listeners.
- **g. Tashkil (to form or to organise).** This act is concerned with the induction of the people into the Jamaat. After the talk, the

speaker requests the people to spare some time for joining the Tablighi Jamaat. People are then requested to spent three chillas at least once in a lifetime, one *chillah* (fourty days) in a year and three days in a month. Thereafter people are persuaded voluntarily to join or spent time with the Jamaat as per their convenience. The names of the people willing to join the Jamaat are then written by one of the members of the group on the diary /notebook. In this way, some people join the Jamaat, and new members are recruited in the group constantly for different periods of time.

In the end, people are requested to organize two *taleems* every day, one in the *mohalla* mosque and the other in their homes. They are also required to attend the weekly ijtema (congregation) of their zonal mosques. This weekly *ijtema* though not common in every zone, is held regularly in some zones.

- **h. Adaab-e-Taam (Etiquette of taking meals).** Before taking the food or meals, a member of the Jamaat is assigned the task of explaining the etiquette of taking meals to all members. All the members sit together on the floor for taking meals. While explaining the etiquette of taking the meals, stress is laid on the fact that every action of the Muslims should be strictly in accordance with the teachings or traditions of the Prophet Mohamad (PBUH). Islam is defined as the complete way of life, where Prophet Mohammad is said to have laid the instructions or etiquette for each and every day to day actions of the Muslims. If the actions of an individual are carried out according to the teachings of the Prophet, he will get enormous rewards for them, be they mundane or religious. It is said to the members that one who will revive one Sunnah, tradition, the teaching of Prophet in the age of corruption would be rewarded equal to that seventy of martyrs in Allah's way.

All members must take the meals together with two or three eating from a common plate. The important norms to be followed at the of eating includes washing of hands before taking the meals, reciting particular dua, eating food from one's own side of the plate, eating in a way that the other person does not feel repelled, cleaning the entire plate and not leaving any food to be wasted. Any negative comment on the quality of the food is avoided. Upon completion of the meal, a dua is recited in gratitude of Allah for taking care of their hunger and thrust by providing them food, including other uncountable blessings.

- **i. Adaab-e-Naum (etiquette of going to bed).** Before going to bed, a member will occasionally repeat to all other members the etiquettes of going to bed or sleeping. This act also has to be performed according to the teachings or practices of the Prophet Mohammad (PBUH). It includes going to the sleeping or bed with *wadhu* that is ritual purity, cleaning/winnowing the bed/ blankets thrice, lying or sleeping on one's right side, putting the hand under the cheek, reciting particular verses of the Quran and reciting another dua at the time of waking.
- **j. Bayaan (talk).** There is another bayaan after the moring prayer called *Namaaz-e-Fajr*. In this *bayaan* or talk, the focus is laid on the six principles of the Tabligh. This talk is delivered by one of the members of the Jamaat as decided in the *Mashwarah*.

The above-mentioned activities comprise the daily activities of the Tablighi Jamaat. All these activities are to be followed by the members of the Jamaat, usually consisting of eight to fifteen persons. In addition to these compulsory activities, there are some other activities performed by the members, which are optional in nature and may be carried out individually. The optional activities are Tahajud (late midnight prayer), special zikr as instructed by the Ameer, recitation of the Quran and reading selected religious books

For effective work of the Tabligh, members are expected to involve people from all walks of life, all classes, and all *beradaris* (clan groups). Moreover, Tablighi Jamaat members should visit Ulema, pious and distinguished people of the locality and seek their favour and guidance in order to facilitate their own preaching work and to involve these people in Tabligh. All it requires is the sincerity of intention. Members are reminded to seek forgiveness from Allah in their actions and be ready to correct their actions, realize their duties and shortcomings.

Footnotes:

[32]. https://en.wikipedia.org/wiki/Tablighi_Jamaat

[33]https://viewsheadlines.com/tablighi-jamaat-nizamuddin-markaz-divides-reformist-movement-maulana-saad-kandhalvi-blamed-17456/.

[34]. (http://tablighijamaattruth.blogspot.com/2016/06/shura-tablighi-jamaat-markaz-nizamuddin.html)

[35]. https://www.daily-sun.com/printversion/details/281347/2018/01/12/Crisis-over-Maulana-Saad-ends

[36]. https://viewsheadlines.com/tablighi-jamaat-nizamuddin-markaz-divides-reformist-movement-maulana-saad-kandhalvi-blamed-17456/.

[37]. https://www.dawn.com/news/1391624

[38]. (http://tablighijamaattruth.blogspot.com/2016/06/shura-tablighi-jamaat-markaz-nizamuddin.html

[39]. this case study was written while on the three-day trip/ participation with the TJ and I was assisted in my interview with Ameer of the touring group, namely Abdul Rasheed Khan (case study no 1, see also see page 156-157 unpublished work/ my thesis-shudhganga research repository)

[40] Mashwara means consultation (see also appendix)

[41]. 'Khidmat' (Serving): In Tablighi parlance, Khidmat refers to 'serving'. More precisely, it refers responsibility of looking after the food requirements of the group, which includes arranging, preparing and serving food for it.

[42]. Taleem (education): In Tablighi parlance taleem refers to reciting/ reading various parts of the recommended literature which includes Quran, Faizil-i-Amaal. It also includes teaching

them about six principles, ablution, namaaz, eating, dressing, sleeping etc on the pattern of Sunnah/Islam. (see also appendex)

[43]. The above various organizational strategies of the TJ were known through my participant observation of the Tablighi Jamaat and interviews

[44]. In my case study/interview, as revealed by Asif Iqbal, Bandipora, Kashmir AMU (case no 16. See page 196-197/ unpublished work/ my thesis).

CHAPTER IV

CONCLUSION AND SUMMARY

Tablighi Jamaat comprises most of the basic Islamist movements of the twentieth century. This movement emerged in the era of the new world order when European and Western powers overthrew the global Islamic Caliphate. It was the time when the concept of nation-states, democracy, and development presupposed and predicated on progressive westernization and secularization of societies became the order of the day. Thus Tablighi movement may also be termed as a part of globalization and extensive world order. Besides, these movements emerged in the wake of conflicting and deteriorating socio-political conditions of Muslims all over the world, in particular India, where Muslims were subjected to colonial oppression and at the hands of the majority community of India. The founder of the movement tried to save and secure the identity of the Muslims from the cultural onslaught of these groups, in the light of true Islam, that is, the Quran and *Sunnah* (acts of the Prophet). He constantly highlighted the threat, that a non-Islamic society posed for those who had only supposedly internalized the Islamic faith. Maulana Ilyas liad stress upon certain routine imperatives (for instance 'six principles') borrowed from the Quran and Hadith for the daily affirmation of Islamic identity.

Unlike the ideology of other Islamic movements like JI, Tablighi Jamaat does not hold political establishment, social order or non-believers responsible for the predicament of the Muslims'. It invariably interprets the existential problems of Muslims are due to the punishment from Allah. Maulana Ilyas, for instance, came to believe that the fall of the Muslims from the heights of power and prosperity was actually Allah's punishment for them. It was because they have strayed from the path of Islam and wrongly left the task of 'dawah' to the *Ulama* alone. The Muslim *Ummah* (worldwide Muslim community), he maintained could regain its lost glory-

Caliphate of God on earth only if every Muslim began to lead his or her life strictly according to the dictates of Islam and constantly engage in its *dawah* (invitation) and *tabligh* (Numani, n.d.). It was each Muslim's religious duty to see himself or herself foremost as *muballig* or missionary of Islam. So reflecting the conflicting socio-political conditions around the world and in particular, India, where Islamic identity and in particular neo-Muslims were under threat of Hindu revivalist movements, Ilyas started his project of *dawah* among the Nau-Muslims of Mewat, who were still retaining many of their age-old customs and traditions, linked with Hinduism (Numani, 1989:21). It is here he devised the ideology of the Tableeghi movement focusing on making Muslims good Muslims, strictly abiding by the dictates of their faith and not on the conversion of non-Muslims (Marwah, 1979). He tried to foster the belief system of the Muslim faith and trust '*Imaan wa yaqeen*' sincerely in one Allah primarily in the light of six principles like '*Kalima, Namaaz, Ilm wa Zikr, Ikram-i-Muslim, Ikhlas-i-Niyat,* and '*Tafrigi Wakt* or *Dawat-i-Illallah*.

It is wrong to believe that this movement merely deals with worship or ritual observances, Ilyas like Maududi (founder of Jamaat Islami) saw Islam as a broader system complete whole' and yearned to revive Islam in its entirety (Sikand, 2002b); at one occasion, he was seen asking Meos to subordinate their trade, *panchayats*, laws or decisions strictly to the injunctions of Quran otherwise their faith would avail them nothing but pure infidelity (Nadwi, 1983); however, he called his work' initial work' stressing on building Muslims strong, so that other things may proceed easily and happily. However, after the demise of Maulana Ilyas, an ideological shift, at least in action, came in the Tableeghi Jamaat, whereby it began to limit Islam to the observance of basic Islamic rituals. Nonetheless, what strikes my mind is difficult to believe how Muslims in general and Tablighi's,, in particular,, could believe only in certain aspects while neglecting some others when they believe in *Kalima Shahadah* that is 'Artice of Faith'. For every Muslim or Tablighi who recites *Kalima Shahadah* or professes faith in Islam, it becomes fundamental for him to believe in Islam in its entirety, the way taught by Prophet Mohammed (PBUH). Thus, when *Kalima Shahadah* is the first principle of the Tableeghi Jamaat's ideological structure, how and why Tableeghi member/s should limit Islam to the observance of only certain basic rituals? Moreover, divorcing Islam in sectors or limiting Islam to basic rituals only would be like believing insincerely in the first principle, that is, '*Kalima Shahadah*'. This makes me believe there could be broadly three factors responsible for their focus on basic rituals, first by following basic rituals strictly by individuals, the other things like institutional or state power will follow easily. It is the individuals who make society or institutions. Second, following basic rituals might have become customary/ritualistic among the members. As the Tablighi members hardly talk about a state or institutional power in their gatherings, so most of the members have taken/imbibed Islam limited to these practice of basic rituals or six principles. Third, it may be pragmatic in nature to avoid any difficulty in their revival work of making Muslims practising, strictly abiding by the dictates of faith. This can be attained only if they remain away from controversial issues in the age of Islam-o-phobia like Jihad or Islamic State. Thus as of yet, TJ focuses on empowering individuals rather than focusing on the empowerment of the institutions of the state.

Tablighi Jamaat could be termed as a fundamental Islamist movement, at least in its ideology, by giving primacy to '*Shariah*' the way it was founded by Maulana Ilyas. However, as in action in its present state, it focuses on empowering individuals by making them practising Muslims. Thus Tableeghi Jamaat follows a bottom-up approach seeking restructuring of societies or institutions starting from the individuals, unlike Jamaati Islami, which follows a top-down approach focusing on restructuring of the societies and institutions by attaining political power of the state at least in the ideology. So it can be said Tablighi Jamaat seeks individualization of Shariah, unlike Jamaati Islami seeking Shariazation of State.

The ideology of the TJ is based on the selective appropriation of Islam as exemplified in the lives of Prophet Mohammad (PBUH) and his companions. This appropriation is codified in both written and oral traditions and is presented in the form of general principles, concepts, symbols and rituals. The general principles of the Tablighi ideology working as an overarching canopy where people from diverse socio-economic backgrounds find meaning in its organizational structure. On the one hand, it stresses upon its followers to develop a sense of shared belongings with reference to *'chai batien'* (six principles) and five pillars of Islam. On the other hand, in its organizational structure, it accommodates diversities of world views, cosmologies, lifestyles, cultures, and people from diverse political orientations. The other noteworthy features of the Tableeghi Jamaat ideology are the importance given to travel and its self-funding, aversion to using of force and violence, focus on humbleness, aversion to politicking, emphasis on the transformation of the individual self rather than the transformations of institutions, state or social order etc.

Unlike the ideology of other Islamists, Tablighi Jamaat does not hold corruption in governing systems, political establishments, institutions, social order or non-believers responsible for the corruption or abject conditions of the Muslims. It invariably interprets the existential problems of the Muslims as due to the punishment from Allah having Muslims have left the fundamentals of Islam. Therefore, the solutions, to the various problems of the Muslims, according to Tablighi ideology, lies in transforming the individual's life and identity in the light of commands of Almighty Allah and Prophet Mohammad (PBUH), not through seizing state power or reform of political institutions. This ideological posture towards politics has led some scholars to call it an apolitical movement. However, orientation to the choices of values and purposes of an individual and society are in themselves political in nature. Moreover, believing sincerely in the *Kalima Shadaha* itself entails the Muslims in general Tablighi's, in particular, to believe in Islam in its entirety as complete religion, without divorcing it into sectors. However, time and context play an important role in the nature and moderation of ideologies of the various movements. Thus Tableeghi Jamaat's various characteristics like aversion to publicity, political issues, focus on the individual self, basic rituals, conversion or purification of Muslims only are relative to time and space yet hold an important position in its ideology in action.

The activities of Tablighi ideology are carried out by the loosely centred organizational structure of the Tablighi movement. The activist's perception and the interpretation of the world are sharpened in the context of face to face interaction, frequent repetition of the schedules and routines of the Tablighi organization. These sharpened and focused perceptions are channelized along with ideological and organizational inputs to the pointed critique of the assumptions, goals, values and culture of conventional society. The organization of Tablighi Jamaat operates at several levels starting from the micro-level of 3 to 12 members of the neighbourhood to the zonal, district, state, national, and international levels. The head of the Jamaat at each level is called 'Ameer. The *Ameer* for basic or micro-levels is appointed at the zonal level. By holding consultations with all the members of the Jamaat, the Ameer allocates various roles to each and every member of the touring group every day. The roles assigned in Jamaat are *Khidmat* for preparing the food and serving food to members; *Aelaan* that is making the announcement after every *namaaz* about the arrival of the TJ and making a request to all persons to stay to listen to a religious talk; *Bayaan* that is religious talk; *Taleem*, that is reading out some portions from Fazail-e-Aamaal; *Ghast* that is taking a round of the neighbourhood and inviting people to attend the *Namaaz* and listen to religious talk; *Tashkeel*, that is to motivate and organize people to opt for the touring preaching Jamaat for various durations and writing down the names of the people willing to join the Jamaats; etiquettes of taking meals, etiquettes going to bed and learning about six principles.

The pattern of role allocation in the organizational structure of the TJ has an ideological basis and significance. By that is meant that the importance of every role in Jamaat is explained with reference to how it was practised by Prophet Mohammad (PBUH) and his companions. Thus the role allocation is not an outcome of a decision by a functionary in power rather is primarily ideological in nature and associated with the teachings of Islam. For instance, *Khidmat,* in a mundane sense, involves cooking food for the members of the Jamaat. But when this concrete act is linked to biographical details of Prophet Mohammad and his companions, then every role becomes virtuous. Similarly, activities like *Ghast* patrolling or travelling, *Dawah* invitation towards Islam; *Bayaan* religious talk; or *Taleem* education are primarily seen as the virtuous acts of Prophet Mohammad (PBUH) and his companions enjoined by the Quranic teachings.

In the era of globalization, especially since 9/11, Islamic movements throughout the world have come under great scrutinization of governments and relevant agencies. Besides, the war of 'western powers' on Islam 'in the name of 'war on terror and the assault of *Hindutva* forces on Muslims on Secularism on democracy in India, has led to a moderation of the ideology of Tableeghi Jamaat. Thus in its present form, Tablighi Jamaat, including Jamaat Islami, are primarily longing for the democracy, secular ethos of the nations and have wholeheartedly embraced them (these ideologies), which otherwise they bitterly rejected (see also, Ahmad, 2009). The Modi-led government has further added fuel to the problem '*Hindutva* assault', including the recent 'barbarous communal violence of Delhi 2020' in which hundreds of Muslims were killed and burned, including their homes, *Masajids,* and religious scriptures. Consequently, he has left no stone unturned in suppressing the Muslims (Zafar and Abdullaha: 2020; Krishna and Das Kumar, 2021).

Tablighi Jamaat, which is blamed as 'playing into the hands of enemies' by various Islamist movements like Jamaat-i-Islami' for its apolitical stance (or 'indifference to political matters of the

Ummah') and its focus on mere rituals, was not even left by *Hindutva*-Modi regime. They were made scapegoats for spreading the 'Corona Virus' by calling it 'Tablighi virus,' and all Muslims were subjected to a rise in violence at the hands of the Hindu regime in power by accusing them of 'Corona Jihaad'[45]'[46]. Even some reputed media outlets published cartoons of coronavirus in Muslim attire, and social media was flooded with messages like 'Muslim virus' and 'terrorists. No stone was left unturned by the mainstream media in vilifying Tablighi Jamaat. Not only had many ruling leaders labelled them of 'corona terrorism', but 'Dara-ul Uloom Deoband' of which it is an offshoot, was also reported advocating bane on it. Consequently, Tablighi gatherings were banned, including foreign Tablighi members for entering India for the next ten years when there were just a few hundred cases of Covid-19; nonetheless, nothing was said about other religious gatherings or recent elections of the Modi/BJP regime gathering thousands and lakhs of people when India is about to cross whopping 10 million Covid-19 cases (Zafar and Abdullaha: 2020; NDTV, 2021). However, more recently, on December 15, 2020, as reported by many media outlets, the Delhi court acquitted all the foreign Tablighi activists (from 14 countries) of false charges related to the spreading of covid-19 (The Hindu, 2021).

In a nutshell, Tablighi Jamaat, in its present form, is the most successful Islamic movement and has further capacity to flourish and survive in a wide range of socio-political environments. However, the time, space, context and political environment of the world will also determine its future course of action.

Footnotes

[45]. Coronavirus exacerbates Islam-o-phobia in India, Times Magazine April 3, 2020. https://time.com/5815264/coronavirus-india-islamophobia-coronajihad/

[46]. 'How the coronavirus outbreak in India was blamed on Muslims'. Aljazeera news, April 18, 2020.

Appendix I Tablighi Jamaat: Organisational Strategies

PIC 1. *MASHWARA* /CONSULTATION

PIC 2. *TALEEM* /READING /EDUCATION

PIC 3. BAYAAN/RELIGIOUS TALK /SPEECH

PIC 4 *KARGUZARI* (WORKING/PROGRESS REPORT)

References

a

1. Agwani, M. (1986). *Islamic Fundamentalism in India*. Chandigarh: Twenty-First Century India Society.
2. Ahmad, I. (2009). *Islamism and Democracy in India: The Transformation of Jamaat-e-Islami*. Princeton: Princeton University Press.
3. Ahmad, I. (2010). Genealogy of the Islamic State: Reflections on Maududi's Political Thought and Islamism. In *Islam, Politics, Anthropology*. https://doi.org/10.1002/9781444324402.ch9
4. Ahmad, M. (1991). Islamic Fundamentalism in South Asia: The Jam'at-i-Islami and the Tablighi Jamaat of South Asia. In M. E. Marty, R. S. Appleby, & S. Asia (Eds.), *Fundamentalisms Observed*. Chicago and London: University of Chicago.
5. Ahmed, R. (1994). 'Identity in South Asia: The Transformation of the Jamaati Islami'. In E. M. and R. S. A. Martin (Ed.), *In Accounting for Fundamentalisms: The Dynamic Character of the Movements*. Chicago and London: University of Chicago.
6. Alam, S. A. Z. M. (1985). *The Message of Tableeg and Da'wa*. Dhaka: Islamic Foundation Bangladesh.
7. Apoorvanand, 2020. "How the coronavirus outbreak in India was blamed on Muslims". Aljazeera News, April 18, 2020, retrieved on August 25, 2021
8. Baliyavi, M. U. (n.d.). *Tarikh-i-Da'wat-o-Tabligh*. Dehli: Arshi Publications.
9. Baliyavi, M. U. (2013). *Tarikh-i-Dawa'at-o-Tabligh*. Dehli: Arshi Publications.
10. Bhatt, S. (2020) 'Lal Ded: Her Spiritualism and Present Scientific World Order', *Kashmiri Overseas Association*. Available at: http://www.koausa.org/lalded2/3.html
11. Bilqies, Shahida (2016), 'Response of the Ulama to Sufi and Reshi Movements in Kashmir in 18th and 19th Centuries' Journal

Of Humanities And Social Science (IOSR-JHSS), Volume 21, Issue 5, PP 64-74.

12. Beckford, J. A. (1983). The Restoration of "Power" to the Sociology of Religion. *Sociological Analysis*, *44*(1), 11. https://doi.org/10.2307/3711656

13. Berger, P. (1967). *The Social Reality of Religion*. Harmondsworth, Penguin Books.

14. Berna, D. D. (2008). A revolutionary perspective on social movements: Fundamentalism in the Islamic world. *ProQuest Dissertations and Theses*, (May), 434. Retrieved from http://search.proquest.com/docview/ 89169174?accountid=14553

15. Blaikie, N. (2009). *Designing Social Research* (second). Cambridge, UK: Polity Press.

16. Brecher, M. (n.d.). Brecher, Michael_The Struggle for Kashmir.pdf.

17. Bulandsahri, M. A. E. (1989). *Six Fundamentals of Tabligh*. New Dehli: Idara-i-Isha'at-i-Diniyat.

18. C. R, K. (1990). *Research Methodology: Methods and Techniques* (2015th ed.). New Dehli: Wishwa Prakashan.

19. Charles, J. A. (1966). The Ideology of Maulana Maududi. In *South Asian Politics and Religion*. Princeton.

20. Cohen, S. P. (2003). India, Pakistan and Kashmir. *India as an Emerging Power*, (December 2001), 30–57. https://doi.org/ 10.4324/9780203009888

21. Delvoie, L. A., & Esposito, J. L. (1998). Political Islam: Revolution, Radicalism or Reform? *International Journal*, *53*(4), 802. https://doi.org/10.2307/40203743

22. Denizen, N. K. (1970). *Sociological Methods: A Source book*. (N. K. Denizen, Ed.). London: Butterworths.

23. Durkheim, E. (1912). *The Elementary Forms of Religious Life* (2008th ed.). London: Oxford University Press.

24. Editore, R. (2018). The Political Thought of Abul Ala Mawdudi Author (s): Elisa Giunchi Published by: Rubbettino Editore Stable URL: http://www.jstor.org/stable/43101492, *59*(2),

347–375.

25. Esposito, J. L. (Ed.). (1997). *Political Islam Revolution Radicalism or Reform?* USA: Lynne Rienner Publishers.

26. Evans, P., & Huntington, S. P. (1997). The Clash of Civilizations and the Remaking of the World Order. *Contemporary Sociology,* 26(6), 691. https://doi.org/10.2307/2654621

27. Falahi, U. F. (1996). *Tarikh-i-Da'wat-o-Jihad Baresaghir ke Tanazur main.* Dehli: Hindustan Publications.

28. Fallahi, U. F (2011), 'Ahyaayi Deen aur Hindustani Ulama', Al-Qalam Publications, Baramula Kashmir.

29. Ferozepuri, M. I. (n.d.-a). *Tabligh ka Muqami Kaam* (2011th ed.). Dehli: Rabbani Book Depot.

30. Ferozepuri, M. I. (n.d.-b). *Tablighi jama'at ki Layi Ranvangi ke Hidayat.* Dehli: Rabbani Book Depot.

31. Ferozepuri, M. I. (n.d.-c). *Tablighi Tehreekh ki Ibtida aur uski Bunyadi Usool.* Dehli: Rabbani Book Depot.

32. Gabariou, Marc (2006), 'What is left of Sufism in Tablighi Jamaat'? *Archives de sciences sociales des religions, p. 53-72*

33. Giunchi, Elisa (1994), 'The Political Thought of Abul A'la Maududi', *Il Politico*

34. Vol. 59, No. 2 (169), pp. 347-375, Rubbettino Editore.

35. Greener, I. (2011). *Designing Social Research: A Guide for the Bewildered.* Los Angeles, London: Sage.

36. Greener, I. (2014). *Designing Social Research: A Guide for the Bewildered. Designing Social Research: A Guide for the Bewildered.* SAGE Publications Ltd. https://doi.org/10.4135/9781446287934

37. Hall, J. R. (2003). Religion and Violence: Social Processes in Comparative Perspective. *Handbook of the Sociology of Religion,* 358–384.

38. Haidar Malik Chãdurãh (1991), Tãrîkh-i-Kashmîr; edited and translated into English 'History of Kashmir' by Razia Bano, Delhi, Bhavna Prakashan.

39. Haq, S. A. (1972). *The Faith Movement of Maulana Mohammad Ilyas.* London: George Allen and Unwin.

40. Haqqani, A. R. (n.d.). *Jama'at me Kyun Jaye?* New Dehli: Nasir Book Depot.

41. Haralambos M and Heald R.M. (1997). *Sociology: Themes and Perspectives*. Oxford University Press.

42. Hasan, M. (1997). *Nationalism and Communal Politics in India: 1885-1930*. New Dehli: Manohar.

43. Hind, J. I. (1958). *Rudad* (2010th ed.). New Dehli: Markazi Maktaba Islami publishers.

44. Hussain, M. A. (n.d.). *Faza'il-i-Miswaaq*. New Dehli: Idara-i-Isha'at-i-Diniyat.

45. IGNOU. (n.d.-a). *MSO 002 Research Methodologies and Methods (Book-2)* (2014th ed.). Dehli.

46. IGNOU. (n.d.-b). *MSO 002 Research Methodologies anf Methods (Book-3)* (2014th ed.). Dehli.

47. Islam, M. (2012). Limits of Islamism: ideological articulations of Jamaat-e-Islami in contemporary India and Bangladesh, (May).

48. Jackson, R. (2010). *Mawlana Mawdudi and political Islam: Authority and the Islamic state. Mawlana Mawdudi and Political Islam: Authority and the Islamic State.* https://doi.org/10.4324/9780203848722

49. Jaques, T (2007), Dictionary of Battles and Sieges: P-Z, Greenwood Publishing Group. Retrieved 8 November 2020.

50. Jamal, A. (2009). Gendered Islam and modernity in the nation-space: Women's modernism in the Jamaat-e-Islami of Pakistan. *Feminist Review, 91*(1), 9–28. https://doi.org/10.1057/fr.2008.43

51. John A. Hannigan. (1991). Social Movement Theory and the Sociology of Religion: Toward a New Synthesis. *Sociological Analysis, 52,* 311–331. Retrieved from https://www.jstor.org/stable/3710849

52. Jones, K. W. (1972). *Arya Dharm: Hindu Consciousness in Nineteenth Century Punjab*. New Dehli: Manohar.

53. Kandhalavi, M. S. (2009). *The Six Numbers*. Hyderabad: Nasir Book Depot.

54. Kandhalawi, E. H. (1989), '*Masulmano ki Pasti Ka vahid Ilaaj*'.

New Dehli: Idara-i-Isha'at-i-Diniyat.

55. kandhalawi, M. Y. (1981). *Hayatus Sahaba.3 vols.* New Dehli: Idara-i-Isha'at-i-Diniyat.

56. Kashmiri, S. N. A. (1979). *Jamaat-e-Islami ke din ka khulasa.* Srinagar: Islamic Publications.

57. Khan, S. A. (n.d.). *Ek Qimati Mashwara.* Punhana: Maktaba Subhaniya.

58. Khan, W. (1986). *Tabligh Movement.* New Dehli: the Islamic Centre.

59. Khan, D. (2018) *Born with Wings: The Spiritual Journey of a Modern Muslim Woman,* New York: Random House.

60. Khawaja, S. B. (n.d.). Ihd Nama Kashmir_Kwaja Sanaullah Bhat.Pdf.

61. Krishna N. & Das, Kumar 2021. "Rallies, Religious Gatherings Aggravate India's Worst Covid-19 Surge" Reuters, April 8, 2021. Retrieved on August 27 2021.

62. Kumar, R. (2005). *Research Methodology- A Step-by-step Guide for Beginners.* London: Sage Publications.

63. Lamb, A. (1967). The Kashmir problem: a historical survey. Retrieved from http://cat.libraries.psu.edu/uhtbin/cgisirsi/0/0/-0/5?searchdata1=%5EC592267

64. Lechner, F. J. (1984). Ethnicity and revitalization in the modern world system. *Sociological Focus,* *17*(3), 243–256. https://doi.org/10.1080/00380237.1984.10570477

65. Lone, Rameez Ahmad (2024). Navigating Islamophobia, COVID-19 bans, and ideology: a study of Tablighi Jamaat's apolitical movement and jihad in a complex world. Cont Islam 18, 501–517, 2024. https://doi.org/10.1007/s11562-024-00565-w

66. Lone, Rameez Ahmad (2024b). Islamic State: Unveiling Abu Ala Maududi's Divine Sovereignty and Political Vision in Colonial India. POLITICON: Journal Ilmu Politik, State Islamic University of Indonesia. Vol. 6 No. 1, 2024. Pp 150-164.

67. Lone, Rameez Ahmad (2023), An Apolitical Islamic Movement in the age of Islamophobia: A Case Study of Tablighi Jamaat

in India Amid the Pandemic COVID-19. The Islamic Quarterly, Islamic Cultural Centre and London Central Mosque, UK. Vol 67, No. 1, pp. 97-117.

68. Lone, Rameez Ahmad. (2021a), Religious Tourism: An Insight into the Islamic Tourism of Tablighi Jamaat. EPRA International Journal of Multidisciplinary Research (IJMR), Vol. 7 (9), 2021, pp. 149-153

69. Lone, Rameez Ahmad. (2021b), Tablighi Movement Of 20th Century: Six Principles. EPRA International Journal of Multidisciplinary Research (IJMR), Vol. 7 (9), 2021, pp. 113-18

70. Lone, Rameez Ahmad. (2021c), *Two Faces of Islamic Movements in Kashmir Valley: A Comparative Study of Jamaat Islami and Tableeghi Jamaat.* Doctoral Thesis, Department of Sociology, Aligarh Muslim University

71. Lone, Rameez Ahmad. (2018a). Jamaat-i-Islami: Ideology, International Journal of Research in Social Sciences, 2018, volume:8(5), 792–798

72. Lone, Rameez Ahmad. (2018b). Tablighi Jamaat: Ideological Structure, International Journal of Research in Social Sciences, 2018, Volume 8(1), 1001–1011.

73. Mahdi, T. (1985). *Tablighi Jamaat: Apne Bane ke Malfuzat ke Aiene main.* Deoband: Maktaba al-emaan.

74. Mamud, Y. A. (2019). Islamism and Social Movement Framework. *Academia Education.*

75. Mangal, S.K and Mangal, S. (2015). *Research Methodology in Behavioural Sciences.* Delhi: PHI Learning Private Limited.

76. *Manshur Jamaat-i Islami, Suba'i Intikhabat Kay Li'ay.* (n.d.) (2009th ed.). Lahore: Shoba'i Jamaat-i Islami Pakistan.

77. Mapril, J., Blanes, R., Giumbelli, E., & Wilson, E. K. (2017). Secularisms in a Postsecular Age?: Religiosities and Subjectivities in Comparative Perspective. *Secularisms in a Postsecular Age?: Religiosities and Subjectivities in Comparative Perspective*, 1–300. https://doi.org/10.1007/978-3-319-43726-2

78. Maqbool, S. (2017). Islamism and Electoral Politics: A Case Study of Jama'at-i-Islami Jammu and Kashmir (1971-87), 7(8),

54–58.

79. Marwah, I.S. (1979). Tablighi Movement among the Meos of Mewat. In *Social Movements in India*. Dehli: Manohar.

80. Masud, K. (2000). *Travellers in Faith: Studies of the Tablighi Jama'at as a Transnational Islamic Movement for Faith Renewal(ed)*. The Netherlands. Brill: Leiden.

81. Maududi, Abul. Ala. (n.d.-a). *Masla-i Qumiyat* (2015th ed.). New Delhi: Markazi Maktaba Islami publishers.

82. Maududi, Abul. Ala. (n.d.-c). *Tarjumanul Quran*. Dehli: Markazi Maktaba Jamaat-E-Islami Hind,1998.

83. Maududi, Abul Ala. (1937). *Maulmaan Aur Maujada Siyasi Khashmakash*. Pathankot: Maktaba Jamaat-e Islami.

84. Maududi, Abul. Ala. (1941). *Qur'an ki chaar bunayadi istelahen*. (A. Asad, Ed.) (2012th ed.). New Dehli: Markazi Maktaba Islami publishers.

85. Maududi, Abul. Ala. *(1941), 'Islami Huqumat Kistrah Qaim Huskti Hai'.New Dehli(7th Edition 2017) Markazi Maktaba Islami Publishers.*

86. Maududi, Abul. Ala. (1967). *Islam ka Nazriya Siyasi* (2015th ed.). New Dehli: Markazi Maktaba Islami publishers

87. Mazhari, Q. (1972). Hazrat Maulana Ilyas Sahib aur Unki Tehrik. In *Kya Tablighi Kaam Zururi Hai?* Mumbai: Faqir Bhai Maniyar.

88. Mc Guire, M. (1982). Pentecostal Catholics: Power, Charisma and Order in a Religious Movement. Philadelphia: Temple University Press.

89. Mc Guire, M. (1983). Words of power: Personal empowerment and healing. *Culture, Medicine and Psychiatry*, 7(3), 221–240. https://doi.org/10.1007/BF00049311

90. Metcalf, B. D. (1982). *Islamic Revival in British India: Deoband 1860-1900*. Princeton: Princeton University Press.

91. Metcalf, B. D. (2003), "Travelers' Tales in the Tablighi Jama`at." Annals of the American Academy of Political and Social Sciences. Vol. 588, Islam: Enduring Myths and Changing Realities, 136-148.

92. Minault, G. (1982). *The Khilafat Movement: Religion and Political*

Mobilisation in India. New York: Columbia University Press.

93. Momin, (2018), "Tahreekh Islami kai Sathr Saal" Vol 2, Srinagar (weekly), Bara Pather, Batamaloo

94. Mukerji, P. N. (2000). *Methodology in Social Research; Dilemmas and Perspectives*. New Dehli: Sage Publications.

95. Mukerji, P. N. and C. S. (n.d.). Conversations with Ramakrishna Mukherjee. In P. N. Mukerji (Ed.), *2000*. New Dehli: SAGE Publications.

96. Nadwi, H. K. I. A. (1986). Main Bhi Hazir Tha Wahan.

97. Nadwi, S. A. H. A. (n.d.). *Ilyas aur Unki Deni Daw'at*. Deoband: Kutub Khana Aizazzi Jamia Masjid.

98. Nadwi, S. A. H. A. (1983). *Life and Mission of Maulana Mohammad Ilyas*. Lucknow: Academy of Islamic Research and Publications.

99. Nadwi, Z. M. (n.d.). *Daw'at-o-Tabligh ke Usul-o-Ahkam*. Deoband: Kutub Khana Aizazzi Jamia Masjid.

100. Naqvi, M. (1978). *Khawaja Hassan Nizami: Hayat aur Adabi Khidmat*. Lucknow: Naseem Book Depot.

101. Nasr, A.-A. (1994). *Imitation of the Kufaar*. Philadelphia: Islamic Propagation, Information and Resource Centre.

102. Nasr, S. W. R. (1996). *Maududi and the Making of Islamic Revolution*. New York: Oxford University Press.

103. NDTV, 2021 "Have Witnessed Such a Rally For The First Time...": PM Modi In Bengal, April 18, 2021. Retrieved on August 26, 2021

104. Niyazi, K. (1974). *Jamaat-i Islami Awami Adalat Main*. (2014, Ed.). Lahore: Maktaba Jamaat-e Islami.

105. Nizami, K. H. (1923). *Da'i-i-Islam*. Amritsar: Roz Bazar Burqi Press.

106. Nizami, M. K. (n.d.). *Paigham-i-Falah* (2016th ed.). Sahranpur: Maktaba Jam-i-Nur.

107. Numani, M. (n.d.). *Malfuzat-i-Hazrat Maulana Muhammad Ilyas* (1991st ed.). New Dehli: Idara-iIsha'at-i-Diniyat.

108. Numani, M. (1989). *Tablighi Jama'at, Jama'at Islami aur Barelwi Hazrat*. Lucknow: Al-Furqan Book Depot.

109. Parsons, T. (1942) 'Age and Sex in the Social Structure of the United States', *American Sociological Review*, 7(5), p. 604. doi: 10.2307/2085686.

110. Perrigo, Billy 2020 "It Was Already Dangerous to Be Muslim in India. Then Came the Coronavirus" Time Magazine April 3, 2020, Retrieved on August 26, 2021

111. Pieri, Z. P. (2015). *Tablighi Jamaat and the Quest for the London Mega Mosque: Continuity and Change (The Modern Muslim World)*. London: Palgrave, Macmillan.

112. Pierre, H. (1987). *"George W.F.Hegel."* (L. S. and J. Cropsey, Ed.). Chicago: University of Chicago Press.

113. Qasmi, M. R. (n.d.). *Ghar ki Taleem* (2015th ed.). Kamalpur: Jamia Arabia Imdad-ul Ulum.

114. Qasmi, M. R. S. (1996). *Bayanat-i-Hajratji Maulna Inam-ul Hassan Sahib*. New Dehli: Makataba al-Ilm.

115. Qasmi, M. S. (1992). *Jamaati Islami aur Tablighi Jmaat main Fraq: Aik Taqabali Jaiza*. Dehli.

116. Redding, J. A. (2011). Islamism and Democracy in India: The Transformation of Jamaat-e-Islami by Irfan Ahmad. *American Anthropologist.* https://doi.org/10.1111/ j.1548-1433.2010.01321_1.x .

117. Reetz, Dietrich. "Keeping Busy on the Path of Allah: The Self-Organization (*Intizām*) of the Tablīghī Jamā'at." *Oriente Moderno* 84.1 (2004): 295–305.

118. Ritzer, G. (1996). *Sociological Theory*. London: Tata Mc Graw Hill.

119. Robertson. R. (1989). "Globalization, politics and religion," In J. B. and T. Luckmann (Ed.). London: Sage.

120. Robertson, R. (1985). The sacred and the world system. In P. E. Hammond (Ed.), *The Sacred in a Secular Age* (pp. 347–358). Berkeley: University of California Press.

121. Rudad Jamaati Islami Hind (2010), New Dehli, Jamai Nagar, Markazi Maktaba Islami Publishers.

122. Saber, Satish and Hassan, M. (2006). *Assertive Religious Identities: India and Europe*. New Delhi: Manohar.

123. Saberwal, S., & Hasan, M. (2006). *Assertive religious identities: India and Europe.* New Delhi: Manohar: Distributed in South Asia by Foundation Books. Retrieved from http://www.loc.gov/catdir/toc/fy0609/2006554474.html

124. Sabir, I. (2015). *The Life and Times of Shaikh Ahmad Sirhindi.* Aligarh Muslim University.

125. Saeed, A. (2006). Islamic thought: An introduction. *Islamic Thought: An Introduction,* 1–204. https://doi.org/10.4324/9780203015247

126. Sardar, Z. (2004). *Desperately Seeking Paradise: Journeys Of A Sceptical Muslim.* London: Granta Books.

127. Sarwar, M. (1956). *Maulana maududi ki Tehrik-i-Islami.* Dehli: Markazi Maktaba Islami.

128. Shakir, M. (1972). *Muslims in Free India.* New Dehli: Kalamkar Prakashan.

129. Shraddhanand, S. (1925). *Andha Ayteqad aur khufia Jihad.* Dehli: Tej Press.

130. Sijapati, M. A. (2012). Mawdudi's Islamic Revivalist Ideology and the Islami Sangh Nepal, *17* (June), 1–21.

131. Sikand, Y. (1997). The Fitna of Irtidad: Muslim Missionary Response to the Shuddhi of Arya Samaj in Early Twentieth Century Nort India. *Journal of Muslim Minority Affairs, 17*(1).

132. Sikand, Y. S. (1998). The origins and growth of the Tablighi Jamaa in Britain. *Islam and Christian–Muslim Relations.* https://doi.org/10.1080/09596419808721147

133. Sikand, Y. (1999). Women and the Tablighi Jamaat. *Islam and Christian-Muslim Relations, 10(9)*(March).

134. Sikand, Y (2000) 'Hazrat Bulbul Shah: The First Known Muslim Missionary in Kashmir', Journal of Muslim Minority Affairs, 20:2, 361-367.

135. Sikand, Y. (2002a). The Emergence and Development of the Jama'at-i-Islami of Jammu and Kashmir (1940s-1990), *36*(3), 705–751. https://doi.org/10.1017/S0026749X02003062

136. Sikand, Y. (2002b). *The Origins and Development of the Tablighi Jama'at (1920-2000).* New Dehli: Orient Longman.

137. Singhanawi, A. A. (n.d.). *Tazkira-i-'Ulama-i-Haq.* Lahore: Makkah Publishing House.

138. Putra, Z. I. (2013). The Tablighi Jamaat Movement Its Ideological Concept and, 16–25. https://doi.org/10.18196/AIIJIS.2013.

139. Syed Wali Raza, N. (1994). *The Vanguard of Islamic Revolution: The Jamaat-e-Islami of Pakistan.* Berkeley: University of California Press.

140. Talib, M. (2000). Construction and Reconstruction of the World in the Tablighi Ideology. In *Travellers in Faith.* Lieden, Boston: Brill, Netherlands.

141. Tariq, A. (1995). Hazrat Maulana Enam-ul Hassan Sahib. *Bang Dara, October.*

142. Tellis, W. M. (1997). The Qualitative Report Introduction to Case Study Introduction to Case Study. *The Qualitative Report,* 3(2), 1–14. Retrieved from https://nsuworks.nova.edu/tqr/%0Ahttp://nsuworks.nova.edu/tqr%5Cnhttp://nsuworks.nova.edu/tqr

143. The Hindu, 2021. "Tablighi case: Court acquits 36 foreigners" December 16, 2020. Retrieved on December 29, 2021.

144. The Wire, 2020. "4,600+ Jurists, Scholars, Actors, Artists, Writers Condemn UP Police's Charges Against the Wire", the Wire Magazine, April 18, 2020. Retrieved on August 26, 2021.

145. Troll, Christian W. (1994), "Two Conceptions of *Daʿwa* in India: Jamāʿat-i Islāmi and Tablīghī Jamāʿat." *Archives de sciences sociales des religions* 39.87,115–133.

146. Usmani, M. T. (1995). *Akabir-i-Deoband Kya The?* Deoband: Zam Zam Book Depot.

147. Varshney, A. (1991). India, Pakistan, and Kashmir: Antinomies of Nationalism. *Asian Survey, 31*(11), 997–1019. https://doi.org/10.1525/as.1991.31.11.00p01057

148. Vellori, A. M. K. (n.d.). *Tehrik-i-Da 'wat-o-Tabligh.* Vellore: Dar-ul -Tabligh.

149. Walter, Arnold Howard (1914), 'Islam in Kashmir.' The Muslim world, volume 4(4), p. 340-352

150. Wink, Andre (2004), Al-Hind- The Making of Indo-Islamic World, Leiden Brill.

151. Weekly, P., & Weekly, P. (2017). Kashmir: The Moment of Truth, *36*(39), 3662–3664.

152. Weekly, P., & Weekly, P. (2019). On the Kashmir Question, *36*(17), 1473–1479.

153. Wuthnow, R. (1980). World Order and Religious Movements. In *Studies of the Modern World System* (pp. 57–75). New York: New York Academic Press.

154. Yin, R. (2004). Case Study Research Study and Methods. *EMA - Emergency Medicine Australasia.* https://doi.org/10.1111/j.1742-6723.2004.00614.x

155. Yousuf, A. (2019) 'An Analysis of Impact of Sufism in Kasmir', *International Journal of Research and Analytical Reviews*, 6:1, 932-935.

156. Zacharias P. Pierri (2015), 'Tableeghi Jamaat And The Quest For The London Mega Mosque'. London UK, Palgrave Macmillan.

157. Zafar Hanan and Shaheen Abdullaha, 2021. "Tablighi Jamaat men held for spreading COVID share ordeal" Aljazeera News March 25, 2021. Retrieved on December 30, 2021.

158. Zainuddin, S. (2000). Economic Internationalization and Islamic Resurgence in India. *The International Scope Review*, 2(4).

159. Zainuddin, S. (2006). Local Roots of Tablighi Jamaat in Orrisa. In M. Saberwal, Satish and Hassan (Ed.), *Assertive Religious Identities* (pp. 145–170). New Dehli.

160. Zainuddin, S. (2020). *Some Aspects of Society and Religious Movement among Muslims "The Case of Tablighi Jamaat in Orissa."* Aligarh, Publications Division, Aligarh Muslim University.

161. Zakkriyya, M. (n.d.). *Dadhi ka Wujub* (2013th ed.). Sahranpur: Kutub Khana-i-Isha'at-ul 'Ulum.

162. Zakkriyya, M. (2015). *Faza'il-i- 'Amaal.* New Dehli: Idara-i-Isha'at-i-Diniyat.

Authors Note

This book has been self-published using the Notion Press platform. While every effort has been made to ensure accuracy, some minor typing errors may have occurred. Additionally, the formatting and design reflect the constraints of self-publishing, which has its own advantages and limitations.

I sincerely thank my readers for their time and interest. I hope the book's simple and lucid presentation has been both engaging and beneficial. Thank you. Allah bless!

"And that man shall have nothing but what he strives for."
— Surah An-Najm (53:39)